THE PROCRASTINATION SOLUTION

92 Great Ways to Overcome Procrastination, Manage Your Time, and Increase Productivity

MAX GOLDWALL

Copyright © 2021

Copyright © 2021 by Max Goldwall. All Rights Reserved.

No reproduction without permission.

No part of this book may be reproduced, transmitted, downloaded, decompiled, reversed engineered, or stored in or introduced into any information storage & retrieval system, in any form or by any means, without expressed written permission of the author.

The scanning, uploading and distribution of this book via internet or any other means, without the permission of the author is illegal and punishable by law. Please purchase only authorized editions and do not participate in, or encourage, piracy of copyrighted materials.

Disclaimer: Author does not assume any responsibility for any errors or omissions, nor does he represent or warrant that the information, ideas, plans, actions, suggestions and methods of operations contained herein is in all cases true, accurate, appropriate or legal. It is the reader's responsibility to consult with his or her advisors before applying any of the information contained in this book. The information included in this book is not intended to serve as a legal advice and author disclaims any liability resulting from the use or application of the contained information.

Contents

Preface

Section I

How To Get Started When It's Really Hard

1. The Dopamine Pattern
2. Reduce the Friction
3. A Paradigm Shift in Perspective
4. The "3-Second" Rule
5. Eight Common Activities That Drain Your Energy
6. The Power of Conservative Initiation
7. From Sleepy to Supercharged
8. A Superior Alternative to Motivation
9. The Strategy To Get Into Productive Mood Within Minutes
10. The Community Advantage
11. Why Is Peer-to-Peer Accountability a Game Changer
12. What Is Professional Expertise and Why It Matters
13. The "First 5-Minutes" Technique
14. The Truth Behind Preparation. Is It Worth the Effort
15. Unreliability of Passion and Emotions
16. The Transformative Power of "Consequence" Exercise
17. The Unpleasant Alternative
18. The Trap of Perfectionism
19. Focus On "What" Instead of "How"
20. The Principle of Calculated Influence
21. The Secret to Unleashing Your Inner Drive
22. The "Catch & Redirect" Technique

Section II
How to Take Consistent Action
23. Forward Momentum
24. "Don't Break the Chain" Technique
25. The Recovery-Management Principle
26. Find Your Biological Rhythm
27. The Power of Inner Equilibrium
28. Let Food Be Thy Medicine
29. The Best Investment for Energy & Focus
30. The Slumber Effect
31. A Secret Energy Reserve That Can Double Your Productivity
32. The Vertical Element
33. The Principle of Time-Acceleration
34. Core of Time Management
35. One Barrel at a Time
36. The Dilemma of Disguised Advancement
37. Discomfort Is Temporary

Section III
What to Do When Your Work Is Uninteresting
38. Diamonds in the Rough
39. An Antidote to Boredom
40. Apply The "W.I.I.F.M." Principle
41. The Bright Side of Challenges
42. Accolades and the Flow of Performance
43. The Element of Time
44. The Uncertain Agreement
45. Seek to Eliminate Complexity
46. The Validity of Boredom Management

Section IV
What to Do When You Get Distracted
47. The Restoration of Willpower Reserves
48. Noncompliance Is Essential
49. Identify the Dimensions of Your Attention Span
50. Build Shelter Against Chaos
51. The Truth Behind Efficiency in a Distracted World
52. How to Avert Perpetual Disorientation
53. The Unforeseen Ally
54. The Psychology of Intrinsic Motivation
55. Weekly Performance Analysis Methodology
56. Monthly Performance Analysis Process
57. The Universal Performance Disruptor at Workplace
58. The Quiet Time: Why, When, and How
59. The Contribution of Personal Analytics
60. Harmonize Scattered Bonds

Section V
How to Get More Done in Less Time
61. The "Now" Element
62. Prerequisite of Unparalleled Performance
63. The Game of Divide and Conquer
64. Cycle of Mental Rejuvenation
65. The "Hardest-First" Technique
66. Implementation of Parkinson's Law
67. Fabrication of Mental Road-Map

Section VI
What to Do When You Are Overwhelmed With Workload
68. Identification of Priorities Using Eisenhower's Matrix

69. Utilize The "A.B.C.D.E." Method
70. The Blueprint for Unflappable Focus
71. The Science Behind 40% Loss in Productivity
72. Employ The "80/20" Rule
73. Strategic Delegation of Nonessentials
74. Process-Centric Fixation
75. The Secret to Deep, Laser-Like Focus
76. How to Use Task-Batching for Maximum Productivity

Section VII
What to Do When You Are Facing Inner Resistance
77. The Essential Rule of Personal Conduct
78. Resistance Equals Priority
79. Identification of Internal Impediments
80. The Language of the Brain
81. Reinforce Constructive Behavior Patterns
82. Accumulating References of Productive Events
83. A Guide to Overcome Failure & Rejection
84. Enhancing Immunity to Unfair Criticism
85. Disregard of Perpetual Demoralization
86. Mitigating Turbulent Emotions
87. Exploring the Therapeutic Effects of Yoga for Productivity
88. Trauma: What It Is, Why It Matters, and How to Heal It
89. The Simplest Way to Boost Focus & Mental Clarity
90. Deep Breathing Technique for Inner Tranquility
91. EFT 101: Abolishing Emotional Impediments to Your Goals
92. Trust the Wait. Don't Be Too Hard on Yourself
Parting Thoughts
About the Author
Your Free Ebook

Preface

Finally, my dream had come true.

I was in college.

It was my doorway to a glorious career. And what's even better, I experienced complete freedom for the first time in my life. I could finally set my own schedule - do the things I liked, when I liked. It was awesome! However, this new freedom came at a very high price.

Something strange started happening. I started putting off everything until later. And I do mean *everything*! If something was not related to entertainment or food, I wasn't interested in it. All of my friends started joking about how I had become such a huge procrastinator.

But I didn't mind my procrastination habit at all. In fact, I loved how things were going. It was party time 24x7... which ended quite abruptly when the dates for my semester exams were announced. I had less than 30 days and was as far away from studying as humanly possible. It started stressing me out. And the stress kept on building with the passing of each day.

I started losing my enjoyment regarding my leisure activities. Chatting with people online, hanging out with my friends, watching movies on my laptop – all started feeling bland and with even a weird vacant feeling, all of a sudden.

I knew I should be studying for my exams. I knew studying was totally critical. But for some reason, I just couldn't make myself sit down and open a book. One morning, I looked at the date and realized there were only seven days left!

My stress then turned into a full-blown panic attack!

I switched off my cell phone, locked my room, and jumped onto my chair. I studied like a crazy maniac. I covered as much as I could in that short time frame. Then exams came, and I got below-average grades.

Needless to say, I was disappointed. Not with my grades. I knew I could have achieved better grades if I had studied more. But, I was disappointed with myself. I didn't study when I *had* the time. My procrastination habit cost me my semester exams. I couldn't believe it! A habit that seemed so harmless turned out to be a wolf in sheep's clothing.

I decided to study 'procrastination.' I wanted to learn everything about it.

It has now been over 15 years since that revelation.

During these 15 years, I have learned a lot about procrastination. For example – why do we procrastinate, what harm can it do, and most importantly, how can we overcome it?

As a result of this decision, I studied the work of top productivity experts like Stephen R. Covey, David Allen, Peter F. Drucker, Jim Rohn, Brian Tracy, and many others. I literally read hundreds of books and countless scientific papers on the topic. I went out of my way to talk with a number of high performing sales executives, CEOs, students, and even athletes about the secret of their extraordinary consistency.

After several years of this research and my own thoughts, a clear picture started to emerge.

This book is a result of studying procrastination for 15 years. I am fully convinced that every person reading it can overcome their procrastination habit – not just for a few days at a time, but for a lifetime. Whether you're a student, entrepreneur, corporate employee, or stay-at-home parent, be prepared to experience an unprecedented boost in productivity.

There are 92 unique techniques included in this book, which are backed by the science and experiences of thousands of people. You will find links to help you with the many studies that validate the effectiveness of the upcoming strategies. You'll get to know when each study was conducted, what was tested, and what were the results? These studies are included specifically for readers who want more details on *why these techniques work*.

While I have included links to various studies, this book is not a research document. It's designed to be accessible and useable for everyone.

Do you *need* to read the research part? Not really. Even if you don't read the studies, you can still use the techniques and gain the full benefits from them. Each one is presented with detailed examples, making it easier to understand and apply.

I am confident that these techniques will bring an end to all your procrastination issues. By using the methods outlined in this book, you will not waste precious time procrastinating on important work. It will become second nature for you to achieve your goals well before the deadline.

The information in this book has the potential to completely transform your personal & professional life, just as it did for me and thousands of other people all around the globe. The faster you apply what you learn, the faster you'll see the results.
So let's not wait any longer. This is the start of a new journey. An exciting one!

It's time to get rid of procrastination permanently.

Section I
How To Get Started When It's Really Hard

"The beginning is the most important part of the work" – **Plato.**

One of the biggest challenges for each of us as procrastinators is – to get started.

You know when you have to do something, but you can't make yourself do it. You cannot start. It is difficult. You can't get yourself to start doing the work. There are always better things that you could be doing instead. Sounds quite familiar, doesn't it?

In your mind, you know you should be doing the work right now. You know it's important, but… you tell yourself, "not right now or in a minute." And then you do something else. Doing anything else feels like a better option than doing that work at the moment. There is always something else to do that would be more fun.

The irony is, even when you are doing the fun thing, you don't enjoy it to the fullest. Because in your mind, you know you should be doing the work right now, but you are watching TV. And so, the feeling of guilt takes over.

Later, you beat yourself up for not doing the work. It lowers your confidence further in yourself. You start getting thoughts like, "how will I achieve the things I want in life when I can't even make myself do the work that I know I should be doing."

When I tell this to my clients, they get shocked. "Can you read my mind?!! That's exactly what I do. How do you know that?"

I was a huge procrastinator myself. And I have worked with enough people to realize that the procrastination pattern is quite predictable. I understand the situation extremely well. I know what we go through.

And what we need to overcome it.

The strategies now coming up are some of the very best at helping you get started. Some of them might seem simple. But their simplicity is one of the reasons why they work so well. Please do not underestimate any one of these. Each has been proven quite effective at helping people get up and start doing the work.

As we go deeper into the book, we'll discuss the underlying reasons behind your procrastination habit. We will get to the root cause and deal with it effectively. That is the only way to get rid of procrastination permanently.

But first, let's start with some quick techniques that you can use right away to spring yourself into action.

1. The Dopamine Pattern

"Know thy enemy"

Before we discuss strategies to overcome procrastination, it's important to know what we are actually dealing with.

You probably don't procrastinate on watching YouTube videos or browsing social media. If you are like me, you could spend hours on these activities, without even needing a break.

But what about doing your taxes? That might be just too exhausting.

How about writing an essay or an article? Doesn't sound too tempting, does it?

We know that reading, going to the gym, working on a project, or finishing a pending task is important, but, we still prefer to watch TV and check out everyone's post on social media. Basically, we waste our precious time by doing things that provide no value in the long run.

Why is that?

What's the reason behind this behavior?

Dopamine

Dopamine is a type of neurotransmitter in the brain that is commonly associated with pleasure. It is often referred to as the *feel-good* chemical. But dopamine is more than that. Dopamine regulates our desire for things.

This is what makes us get up and do stuff. To demonstrate how much dopamine affects our behavior, let's look at a breakthrough study on the subject.

In the 1950s, the psychologists - James Olds and Peter Milner did an experiment on the dopamine effect on rats. The rats were put in a chamber that had a special lever. If the rats would press that lever, it would deliver a direct stimulation to their brains, triggering a release of dopamine (which felt really good). What resulted was possibly the most dramatic experiment in the history of behavioral neuroscience: Those rats would press the lever up to 7,000 times per hour to stimulate their brains. This was a pleasure center - a reward circuit - the activation of which was much more powerful than any natural rewards they could get.

A series of successive experiments revealed that rats preferred the dopamine release over food (even when they were hungry) and water (even when they were thirsty). Male rats would completely ignore a fertile female and would repeatedly cross the electrical-shock-delivering floor to reach the dopamine lever. Female rats would abandon their newborn babies to continually press the lever. Some rats would press the lever as often as 2000 times per hour for 24 hours, ignoring all other activities. They had to be taken out of the chamber to prevent death by self-starvation and their obsession. Pressing that lever became their entire world.

Dopamine affects your behavior at the most basic level. For example, you would assume that it is hunger that motivates you to go to the fridge and grab something to eat. That's not entirely true. Even something as basic as getting food and water is regulated by dopamine to a large extent.

In the dopamine experiment above, the researchers then blocked the dopamine release in the rat's brains. That led to demonstration of another strange behavior by the rats. In the absence of dopamine, the rats lost motivation to do anything. They wouldn't even move to get food and water. If the food was placed in their mouth, they would eat it. But they couldn't motivate themselves to get the food.

While this experiment might seem interesting and scary at the same time, it revolutionized the way we look at pleasure, motivation, and dopamine.

Because our brain LOVES dopamine, it pays a lot of attention towards activities that release dopamine in high amounts. If an activity releases a lot of dopamine, you feel a strong 'urge' to do it repeatedly. For example, activities like drinking alcohol, playing video games, and browsing top social media sites trigger high measures of dopamine in the brain. That is why you find them so enjoyable and want to do them again. On the other hand, activities that do not trigger high amounts of dopamine are ignored by the brain. This manifests as thoughts such as - "I don't feel like doing that right now." Sadly, most activities that are beneficial for us trigger low amounts of dopamine. Things like reading, studying, working on a project report, and even completing house chores only release a low amount of dopamine. That is why you don't feel a great motivation to do them.

Dopamine Tolerance

There is another fundamental aspect of dopamine that we should discuss. There is a system inside the human body that maintains chemical and physiological balance. This system is called homeostasis. The chief aim of this particular system is to ensure that all body functions are operating in their desired state and levels. Let's take an example. Our body tries to maintain a body temperature of 37 degrees Celsius or 98 degrees Fahrenheit. Whenever the temperature rises above this mark, the body releases sweat to cool itself down to the optimum temperature. When the body temperature drops below 98 degrees Fahrenheit, we start shivering to produce heat.

The human body is very adaptable. Sometimes, it achieves balance through increased tolerance to external factors. For example, if a person never smoked cigarettes, they will experience an intense reaction to the nicotine, the very first time they smoke. But a regular smoker doesn't feel a thing even after going through an entire pack. The body of a regular smoker has developed an increased tolerance towards smoking.

The same thing happens with dopamine. If you continuously pursue high dopamine activities, your brain will develop tolerance to high levels of dopamine. It will become the new 'normal'. Now you would need to do more of it to *feel good*. For example, suppose you recently started spending time on social media (which is a high dopamine activity). Initially, you would feel amazing even after just spending ten minutes browsing through social media. Over a period of time, your body will develop a tolerance to the high levels of dopamine and now you will need to spend hours on social media to feel as good as before. The more time you spend on it, the more tolerant you become, and then, the more you will need to do it to feel good. It's a continuous cycle.

As a side effect of being accustomed to high dopamine activities, you would have very little motivation for activities that release low amounts of dopamine. Unfortunately, most of the activities that are good for us fall under this category. Things like reading a book, studying for exams, working on a side business, finishing a project report, to even mowing your lawn fall under low-dopamine activities. If you are habitually watching online videos & movies, playing video games, drinking alcohol, or scrolling through different posts on social media, your brain is already accustomed to high dopamine activities. It's very likely that you might find it quite difficult to motivate yourself. Things like work, study, or exercise will not feel interesting or enticing for you.

While you know these things are beneficial and should be done regularly... but, you don't do it or you can't be bothered to do it. Right?

It all comes down to dopamine. It is the reason behind this behavior.

If you don't do something about this hidden problem, you might not see the *permanent* change you are looking for. So, the question is – Can we do something to take back control?

Yes you can!

You can let go of time-consuming bad habits. What's more, you will start finding the low-dopamine activities interesting again.

One of the best ways to reset your brain is to abstain from all high dopamine activities for a period of time. It will help the dopamine receptors in your brain to recover and slowly get back to their normal state. This is called a **dopamine fast**.

This concept was popularized by California psychiatrist Dr. Cameron Sepah. The **dopamine fast** is based on the principles of *cognitive-behavioral therapy* which is widely considered as the gold standard for compulsive behaviors like internet & social media addiction.

Here's what you need to do. Set aside a period of time during which you'll stay away from all high-dopamine activities like drinking alcohol, sex, browsing the internet or social media, playing video games, watching TV, watching online videos, stimulating food, listening to music, etc. The duration of dopamine fast could be anything from one hour to a whole week. It is up to you to decide how long you want to do it. I would recommend starting slowly and gradually increasing the time period. For example, start by abstaining from all high stimulating activities for a few hours at the end of the day. Once you become comfortable with this, do it for one day a week (i.e., every Saturday). Gradually keep increasing the duration as you see fit. But, make sure it is not significantly disrupting your daily routine in any way.

The point is to let your brain take a break from all highly stimulating activities and let it recover. During the dopamine fast, you can still do low-dopamine activities like reading, journaling, taking a walk, talking to people, and reflecting on your thoughts.

Now as you can imagine, you'll feel bored on these days. Your brain is accustomed to stimulation and when you take a break, it will feel boring. But this boredom is actually good for you. It will reduce the sensitivity of the brain's main dopamine receptors and allow your brain to get used to the lower natural amounts of dopamine.

It is comparable to a full body detox that is popular today. In the full body detox, we eat only rejuvenating foods and stay away from harmful foods & drinks. The **dopamine fast** works on similar principles but focuses on recovering the brain from addictive habits of requiring high dopamine levels.

It should be noted that everything we do releases dopamine in some amount. Even taking a shower releases dopamine (albeit very little). It's not that dopamine is bad. Dopamine is important as it assists in motivating us to do things. Our aim should be to reduce the number of activities that produce unnaturally high amounts of it and which create unwanted behaviors.

To conclude this section, it's extremely difficult to feel motivated to work or study when your brain is so distracted by high dopamine activities. We need to reduce the exposure to intense stimulation. It allows our brain to reset and start finding interest in less-fun-but-more-important tasks. So, if you find yourself procrastinating a lot, start the **dopamine fast** as soon as possible. You will feel more focused and motivated to achieve those tasks that have been put aside.

It forms the basic foundation for overcoming procrastination and lack of motivation. Sometimes, the dopamine fast would be enough to resolve your procrastination issue by itself. After this, we can move on to the specific techniques to overcome procrastination.

Now, you can use the upcoming techniques without doing dopamine fast if you want. They work well even by themselves. But if you want quicker results, you should do the dopamine fasting in combination with the upcoming techniques.

With that said, let's move on to the techniques.

2. Reduce The Friction

The Problem

For a procrastinator, getting started is the toughest part. Taking the first step feels quite daunting. So what can we do about it?

The Procrastination Solution

One technique that works wonders is to make it easy for you to actually start. If you are having a difficult time getting started, then design a method to make it easy for yourself to take that first step. Let's look at a few examples.

A student is procrastinating about doing their homework. They want to start studying but can't get themselves to do it. What should they do?

They should make it as easy as possible for them to sit down and start studying. They should set aside time only for study. So they don't have to think too much about when to study. The mobile phone is a major source of distraction. Put it away or keep it on silent mode. The table and chair should be set in place and must be comfortable. If they study on a laptop, it should be at the study table not studying while lying on a bed. They should silence all notifications on the laptop and tell all their friends not to disturb them during study time. Lock the door if need be.

Basically, remove every obstacle that could come between them and studying.

This technique can also be used to complete any work or even those chores that you have been avoiding. If you want to start a business but can't seem to find the energy to do it, or if you are an executive who is struggling to start working on a project report, or even if you are avoiding mowing the lawn; making it easy for you to start can be immensely helpful.

This technique is also quite effective at forming new habits.

For instance, if you want to start jogging in the morning, keep your running shoes & clothes near your bed. It will save you half an hour looking for everything. Finding things get tedious and may cause you to second guess your decision to start jogging. Put your gear near the place you sleep. Just get up, get changed, and go!

Why Does It Work?

According to science, all living organisms are biologically wired to minimize energy expenditure. The greater the energy required to do something, the more we try to avoid it. Would you like to take the lift to the 12th floor or would to take the stairs? Exactly.

We prefer to spend most of the time doing things that are easy and convenient. For example, we could spend hours browsing social media, watching online videos, reading a novel while lying on the sofa or bed. We prefer to order things online and get them delivered to our door. And it makes sense. We want to conserve time and energy, just like every other living creature on earth. It's a survival mechanism. Any species that doesn't try to conserve energy doesn't survive for too long.

You might be thinking, then why is it that some people can do super hard things? How can some people climb on Mount Everest, keep working for decades to build a billion-dollar business, or even train for years to win an Olympic gold medal?

I agree. The human potential is limitless. We are capable of performing extraordinarily hard feats. Absolutely....! But not every day....! Some days you won't have the energy or the motivation to push hard. During these days, this technique would be immensely helpful. By making it easier to get started, you'd avoid wasting your mental and physical energy. As a result, you won't feel a strong inclination to avoid taking action. You won't second-guess your decision. Starting any work becomes smooth and easy.

> *"If you want to make an easy job seem mighty hard, just keep putting off doing it"* – **Olin Miller**.

Summary

- Lower the entry barrier.

- Remove all obstacles between you and the intended work.

- Make it convenient and comfortable.

3. A Paradigm Shift In Perspective

The Problem

Your thoughts are quite powerful. The way you use your thoughts can make or break your day. I am sure you have been through a time when one bad thought in the morning ruined your entire day. Thoughts significantly affect our work life and the amount of work we can get done in a day. For instance, you are feeling tired and not in the mood to do a pending task. Then you say to yourself, *"oh, that work is pending. I have to do it"*.

The more you say that the more your mind will try to resist it. A few moments later, you may end up not doing the work at all.

This phenomenon is called *mental resistance*. It occurs especially when you are mentally or physically exhausted. If you are not in the mood to begin a task, then forcing yourself by thinking, "I have to do it" will create even more resistance.

Sometimes, you can force yourself to do the work by using sheer willpower. But if you're *really* not in the mood to take action or very tired, your willpower would not be enough. Even worse, forcing yourself may make the resistance even stronger.

The Procrastination Solution

Here's a technique that worked very well for many of my clients. Our resistance is born out of the way we think. So that is how we must deal with it. Here's what you can do to get rid of the resistance:

Reframe your thought from *"I have to do it"* to *"I want to do it."*

Try this now. Think of any pending work that you have been procrastinating on, and say to yourself, *"I have to do it,"* and notice how you feel. You feel a lot of resistance. You will not want to do it.

Now - for the same work - say to yourself, *"I WANT to do it."* Notice how much relaxed you feel. There is almost no pressure. You feel like you *can* do it now.

Why Does It Work?

This psychological technique is quite effective in dealing with mental resistance. It tricks your mind into believing that the work is something that we WANT to do, instead of HAVE to do. It releases a lot of inner tension that had been building up. You'll feel an immediate sense of relaxation.

There'll be no pressure of any kind. In this calm state, you and your mind would be on the same page. The only thing left is to get up and start working.

It's easy, quick, and effective. You can use it anytime, anywhere. Try this technique whenever you are thinking, *"I have to do it,"* but can't make yourself get started. And notice how fast it turns things around for you.

"Mastering others is strength. Mastering yourself is true power."
– **Lao Tzu.**

Summary

● When procrastinating, change your thought from *"I have to do it"* to *"I want to do it."*

● Changing thought patterns releases inner tension and makes it easier to get started.

4. The "3-Second" Rule

The Problem

It has been placed on record (and based on research) that an average office worker spends around 51% of the time managing information at the office. That means only 49% of the time is allotted to doing the actual work.

I encourage preparation. I recommend being well-prepared. But there is also something as too much preparation. Some people call it *paralysis-by-analysis*. You might be spending much more time in preparation than you should.

It is one of the worst encouragers of procrastination. When you dedicate so much time to analyzing a particular situation or scenario or task, you expend precious time. That's one serious encourager. Another is that you will most likely be able to see the downsides and risks of such a project while closing your eyes to potential benefits. This might prevent you from starting at all, which it often does.

The Procrastination Solution

Instead of over-analyzing each and every thing that could happen, it is better to be *reasonably* prepared and start taking action. You can deal with whatever comes up later. Start the work and make adjustments as you go. But what if you are accustomed to preparing more than you need to? How do you break out of that habit?

Let me introduce you to a concept called *the 3-second rule*.

If you have a task but can't make yourself do it, then start counting up to three in reverse – 3... 2... 1 and just GO at 1....!

For example, suppose it's time to go to the gym but you are watching TV and cannot make yourself get up. Apply the 3-second rule. First, sit straight. And then count 3... 2... 1...! Go!

Tip 1 – For some people, it works better when they count 3-2-1 out verbally. For others, counting in the mind is enough. Try both to see which works best for you.

Tip 2 – Keep your focus on the numbers while counting. It diverts your attention away from all the negative thoughts and puts it in the present moment. Thus, making it quite easy to take action.

This technique is quite versatile. It works well whether you are procrastinating on:

- Going to a doctor for a routine check-up.
- Doing your taxes
- Writing a thesis/long reports
- Doing your homework
- Cleaning the dishes

You'll be surprised how effective this technique is in making you get started. Here is the science behind it.

Why Does It Work?

According to psychology, people show two fundamental behaviors when they want to achieve a goal:

1. Assessment self-regulation: They deeply analyze the situation and try to find the best course of action.

2. Locomotion self-regulation: They go ahead and take action to achieve it.

Both are important and may be required at different times. The procrastination problem arises when people have a bias towards assessment self-regulation. It leads to overthinking and over-analyzing. Here's when the 3-second rule comes into the picture. It pauses your "over-analysis mode" and puts you right into the action. Because of its short time frame (three seconds), your mind doesn't get time to overthink the situation. You jump straight into the action.

Check out the below links to studies on self-regulation modes if you wish to learn more about it.

https://www.ncbi.nlm.nih.gov/pmc/articles/PMC4389278/

http://www.tpmap.org/wp-content/uploads/2014/11/19.4.1.pdf

Whenever you face problems in starting a task, use the 3-second rule and GO! It is based on sound psychological principles that make you act fast. When used often, it can help you form a habit of taking action quickly, thereby making overthinking and overanalyzing things which may not be of any assistance or from past memories.

Now you have another potent tool in your repertoire of skills against procrastination. Remember to use it often!

> *"We are what we repeatedly do; excellence, then, is not an act, but a habit."* **–Aristotle.**

Summary

- A quick and easy technique to overcome analysis-paralysis is counting 3-2-1 and just MOVE!

- It takes your focus from *"what could go wrong"* to the present moment allowing you to act quickly.

5. Eight Common Activities That Drain Your Energy

The Problem

Have you ever felt like you don't have enough energy to get started? You might feel confused, zoned out, or tired. It would be difficult to handle challenging tasks in this state. More often than not, you end up postponing the work.

The Procrastination Solution

There are some activities we consider are relaxing, like watching TV or random videos on the internet. In reality, they numb your mind and slowly drain your energy. For instance, think about how you feel after watching TV for three or four hours? I feel like something has sucked the life out of me. It becomes so hard to get yourself to do something productive afterwards.

These activities may appear to be relaxing on the surface but do just the opposite. We slowly become more exhausted and unable to perform at our highest capacity. Let's look at another instance. After doing work for some time, many people like to take a break and browse social media to relax. What actually happens is they get even more mentally exhausted. Their mind gets foggy. Their thinking gets befuddled. They lose all their energy towards doing anything afterwards. In this state, work is the last thing they want to do.

These mind-numbing activities are the silent killers of productivity. They are energy-drains disguised as a relaxed, fun time. Here are a few common ones to be careful of:

• Watching TV or random online videos.

- Watching the News (nothing but negativity and drama).
- Sitting at your computer for a long time
- Playing video games
- Browsing social media
- Having lots of sugar and/or simple carbohydrates in meals (the energy crash you get afterwards is massive)
- Alcohol
- Thinking negative thoughts or worrying

These types of activities drain your energy; therefore, making it harder for you to work efficiently. Once you start feeling tired, you want to (or choose to), keep doing these activities because you are too drained to do anything else.

What the Science Says?

In the report *"Television addiction is no mere metaphor,"* Researchers **Robert Kubey** and **Mihaly Csikszentmihalyi** wrote – "What is more surprising is that the sense of relaxation ends when the (TV) set is turned off, but the feelings of passivity and lowered alertness continue. Survey participants commonly reflect that television has somehow absorbed or sucked out their energy, leaving them depleted. They say they have more difficulty concentrating after viewing than before. In contrast, they rarely indicate such difficulty after reading. After playing sports or engaging in hobbies, people report improvements in mood. After watching TV, people's moods are about the same or worse than before."

Here is the link to the full report:
https://www.simpletoremember.com/vitals/TVaddictionIsNoMereMetaphor.pdf

Be careful with these activities. Most of them are like quicksand, the more you engage, the deeper you sink, and the harder it becomes to climb up and out. They are often masked as a relaxed, fun experience. You have to be careful. If you are not sure about whether an activity is energy-draining or not, test it.

Do the activity for one or two hours and notice how you feel afterwards. Look for the below:

- Unable to concentrate on challenging tasks.
- Mentally and physically exhausted.
- Feeling hungry.
- Feeling lazy and unmotivated.

If you experience any of the above, then that activity is most probably draining your energy without you knowing about it. It is recommended that you replace it with something better.

Try to make changes in your lifestyle based on the above discussion. Avoid activities that secretly deplete your energy. Your productivity will get a huge boost. You will feel more alive and vibrant. You will be more engaged and, best of all; you will feel happy for most of your day.

Isn't that something we all want?

> *"Bad habits are like chains that are too light to feel until they are too heavy to carry."* – **Warren Buffet**, CEO, Investor, philanthropist.

Summary

- Feeling exhausted is one of the most common reasons behind procrastination.

- Avoid activities that drain your mental and physical energy.

6. The Power Of Conservative Initiation

The Problem

Great things take time. That's not a quote that's the reality.

One of the biggest sources of discouragement and the one factor that may derail you from taking action is requesting too much from yourself. If you seek massive results in a concise amount of time, it's probably not going to happen.

For example, when you first start to implement the techniques mentioned in this book, you will notice that the process is erratic, unstable, and non-linear. You must expect that. One day, you'll be firing on all cylinders and get a lot done. On other days, you will see yourself not getting to do anything concrete.

That is normal at the beginning. In fact, you should consider it a sign of progress. Some experts have called this constructive laziness or constructive procrastination. What you should not allow, however, is to let it get out of hand. For instance, you perform well for two days and then relapse for three, four days, or more. That's retrogression. So be careful.

The Procrastination Solution

This is where starting small could be helpful. It takes less energy and time to start with smaller steps. You won't get confused or overburdened. It will be easier, to begin with, and also be consistent. Once you gain experience, gradually increase the workload.

For instance, don't try to change your entire diet overnight if that's overwhelming. Start small. Just switch to green tea in the morning. Then, gradually keep adding more healthy food types.

Taking baby steps is a much better option than getting overwhelmed and quitting.

Example #1. Suppose your goal is to lose your belly fat and get in shape. Your action plan could be:

1st step – Join a gym

2nd step – Get familiar with exercises (hire a trainer if needed.)

3rd step – Start working out 5 times a week (or as needed.)

4th step – Gain information about what to eat and what to avoid.

5th step – Start eating healthy.

6th step – Keep improving your workout and diet.

And so on.

Example #2. If you want to improve the marketing of your business, a possible action plan could be:

1st step – Read four marketing books this month.

2ndstep – Consult a top marketing expert in your field.

3rd step – Understand your niche better (study competitors, do a survey, etc.)

4th step – Contact and set up meetings with your marketing people.

5th step – Test a new marketing strategy in the next four weeks.
And so on.

Small actions are the key to getting started. On the same note, be careful when making your schedule for the day. Don't bog yourself down with too many activities. It may be too overwhelming. Just a few – let's say three, will do. When you complete them, you will feel pumped up for more. Gradually you get better and expand to five, then seven and more.

What is even better is that small yet steady improvements tend to stick over the long period of time. Too many changes at once often won't work as intended. The popularity and effectiveness of the KAIZEN approach is proof of that.

Remember, the goal is not to change overnight. The goal is to start and be consistent every day. That is what we want to achieve.

What about Mindset?

Some people ask, *"What about my goals? Should I also keep my expectations reasonable as well?"*

Not really. Thinking big is the reason we advance not just as individuals but as a society. From climbing Mount Everest to landing on the moon, every extraordinary human achievement is made possible only through thinking big. Your thoughts should be revolutionary, massive, and should be matched together with equally bold strides. However, if you are finding it too overwhelming, especially in the beginning, then it's better to start with small steps. You'll be more consistent. As you become more comfortable, then you can increase the workload.

Exceptions to the Rule:

If you are already quite experienced or comfortable with the nature of the task, then starting small is not necessary. Let's take a real-life example. Oliver joined a gym when he moved to a new city. A gym instructor told him to start with lightweight dumbbells as heavyweights are quite demanding on the body. But he began with medium weights and moved to heavyweights within a month. How did it happen?

The gym instructor didn't know that Oliver was not a novice. He was lifting heavy weights for almost a decade. To focus on his finances, he took one year break from the gym. While he didn't look huge, his body was quite accustomed to lifting heavyweights. So when he joined the gym, he said he didn't feel the need to start with ultralight weights. He was fine with slightly heavier weights. But, for a complete beginner, that would be too overwhelming. Lightweights are the better option.

Ultimately, it is your decision to start small or not. Ask yourself - "how comfortable am I with the task at hand?" If you have some experience under your belt, then use your judgement. But if you are doing something for the first time, starting with small steps is recommended. It will be easier to get started and be consistent. Do not underestimate this strategy because of its simplicity. Often, it is the small things that make the biggest difference. You may be pleasantly surprised.

> *"Never underestimate small steps. The man who moves a mountain begins by carrying away small stones."* – **Confucius**, Chinese philosopher

Summary

- Small steps make it easier to get started.

- Small, consistent steps over a period of time can lead to remarkable results.

7. From Sleepy To Supercharged

The Problem

In many instances, you procrastinate because you feel dull and sleepy right after a meal. Normally, it happens after lunch but can occur after a heavy breakfast as well. You would have experienced it many times. You end up feeling lethargic and in a foggy state of mind. In this state, you can only do tasks that don't require a lot of concentration or creative thinking. That is why top CEOs like Jeff Bezos schedule critical meetings in the morning. You tend to have more energy and focus at the start of the day.

So, it is recommended to help with creative thinking; to schedule all your critical work in the morning. But what if you have a challenging task right after lunch?

The Procrastination Solution

Here's a quick but important tip to deal with this situation:

"Eat only till 50% - 80% of your stomach capacity... when you need to be mentally sharp and highly productive right after the meal."

It has been known for generations but is well worth repeating – a full stomach makes you dull. Sometimes we end up procrastinating because we are feeling dull, lazy, and tired. It mostly happens in the afternoon, right after lunch.

It happens because digesting food is one of the most energy-demanding processes for our body. When we eat a heavy meal at lunchtime, our body spends a huge portion of our energy on digesting food. This causes a person to feel lazy, tired, and dull for hours after the meal. Coffee can help a little, but here's a better alternative: at lunch, stop eating "before" your stomach feels completely full. Eat till your stomach is half full.

Now, don't skip your meal altogether as hunger can distract you from performing at your best. Strive for a balance. You should neither be hungry nor completely full.

But how do you find this sweet spot?

Pay attention to your stomach while you are eating. You will observe that there's a point at which you are not hungry anymore. This is the sweet spot. If you keep eating, you'll be completely full which will make you dull afterwards. In the sweet spot, you'll neither be hungry nor completely full. And it's very easy to spot. You only have to pay attention a few times. Soon, you will develop an intuition for it. It will become second nature for you.

Now, let's discuss its benefits. You will immediately feel that you are mentally alert and full of energy. There will be no mental fog or dullness. You'll feel awesome and ready to take on difficult, mentally challenging tasks even during the afternoon. This one is a favorite among many of my clients, mainly because of how simple and effective it is. They always apply it when they have challenging tasks in the afternoon and cannot afford to be dull & sleepy. I always use it when I am writing a book or have a meeting/online session with a client in the afternoon. It allows me to work with maximum focus and efficiency.

My Personal Experience

Let me share a true story. I used to eat a heavy breakfast in the morning, which included bread, milk, sprouted beans, eggs, etc. I thought it was quite healthy because it contained all the necessary nutrients. But there was a small problem.

I just couldn't concentrate on work from morning till mid-afternoon. It was like being in a haze. My focus was all over the place. I couldn't think properly. I felt like a thick fog was covering my brain.

After reading a TON of books and studies, I decided to switch to a green shake in the morning. It contained green leafy vegetables, nuts, essential oils, and some fruits. As you can probably guess - it tasted bad at first, but I experimented with different fruits and got a combination that tasted really good.

After drinking it, I was not completely full but not hungry as well. So it was a nice balance. Now for the important part- from the FIRST DAY I switched from heavy breakfast to a green shake, my mornings got completely transformed. My mind became crystal clear and focused. I could now properly concentrate on an activity without getting disturbed by random thoughts. I could now do the same amount of work in half-day that used to take me an entire day.

Sounds amazing, right? It was a revelation for me too. I always knew that the quality and quantity of food is important, but never expected results to be this dramatic.

"Life is really simple, but we insist on making it complicated." – **Confucius**, Chinese philosopher.

Summary

- Eat 'light' when you have a challenging task after the meal.

- You'll have a lot more energy and alertness.

8. A Superior Alternative To Motivation

The Problem

To get started on a task, we tend to depend too much on motivation. We try many things; we write down our goals, watch motivational videos, read inspirational stories of successful people, and put ourselves in the company of motivated individuals. While these things are beneficial, they do not work as intended because of a basic foundation problem – Motivation is an emotion. Emotions are fleeting. They come and go.

But can we depend on something which is unstable by its very nature? Suppose you are running a company. Would you give a critical work responsibility to an employee who tends to take frequent days off? You wouldn't because he is not dependable. You cannot trust him with those types of essential responsibilities for work.

Then why do we chase motivation - which being an emotion - is highly unreliable? You are motivated one moment; the next, you are not. Is it right to depend on motivation alone?

The Procrastination Solution

Fortunately, there are better options. One amazing technique is called *shaping our environment*. It can help us overcome procrastination and get started on the task – without needing motivation or willpower.

Here's what you should do:

1. Remove the things that distract you from work.
2. Include the things that make it easy to get started.

Let's look at some examples:

Example #1 – Your phone is probably the biggest source of distraction. Constant notifications, calls, messages, and apps immediately highjack your attention and distract you for hours. If your phone is in your immediate workspace, you probably wouldn't be able to concentrate on work. Put it on silent mode and keep it outside your room or in a drawer.

Just the absence of your phone can boost your productivity. When you don't have access to myriads of apps and notifications on your phone, you'll be free to focus on important things like work, exercise, studies, spending time with family, reconnecting with old friends. There are so many wonderful things out there that are often ignored because we are preoccupied with the trivial digital stuff which fills our lives.

The main idea behind shaping your environment is to eliminate things that don't serve you. And keep only the things that help you to take the right actions.

Example #2 – Suppose you want to lose weight and need to stop having sugar. Start by removing all foods containing sugar in your house. Take out all cookies, ice creams, pastries, candies. Replace them with healthier alternatives like cinnamon, carrots, apples, etc.

If you have access to 'bad' options (like pastries when you are trying to quit sugar), you'd depend on willpower to resist it. And that's a problem. The willpower fluctuates at different times of the day. Most people tend to have more willpower in the morning. But as the day goes on, the stress takes a toll on the body and mind. Our self-control weakens. That is why it's harder to resist temptations at the end of the day.

Resource: Read *"The Willpower Instinct"* by Kelly McGonigal for more details on willpower fluctuations.

Suppose you have a grueling day at work and come back home late at night, completely exhausted. In this state, you probably won't stop yourself from going to the fridge and getting a generous helping of pastries. That one action can undo all of your days' worth of weight loss progress.

But what if you don't keep any sweets in your house? Now, when you come back home tired, you won't be able to eat sugar no matter how much you want to. Because the only available options are apples and carrots (as you can guess by now, apples and carrots are my favorite snacks.)

This time, you'll maintain your weight loss progress. You won't depend on motivation or willpower. Both may work in the short term. But if we talk about long term commitment and focus, shaping the environment is the better option. It doesn't fluctuate like motivation or willpower. It is highly reliable as it never changes by itself. We have to manually change it. You'll never find sugar in your kitchen until you buy some and put it there.

The same applies to productivity. Take note of everything that tends to distract you from work. Remove them from your workspace.

- Switch off all notifications on your phone and PC.

- Close the windows and use earplugs if you live in a noisy neighborhood.

- Tell your friends not to disturb you during work.

- Put your phone away when you are working.

It's the same idea. Keep the things that help you get started. Remove the distractions.

It is a powerful strategy that can help you achieve what you want. Flexibility is one of its core strengths. It's not just limited to overcoming procrastination. You can use it to achieve any goal you may have – losing weight, changing bad habits, studying, writing a book/thesis – just to name a few.

Whatever your goals may be, shaping your environment should be an integral part of your action plan. And I firmly believe it's an absolute must for improving productivity.

"One of the best ways to make changes in your life is to change your environment. This then changes you." – **Robert Kiyosaki**, American businessman and author of the *Rich Dad* series.

Summary

- Take note of everything that distracts you from work.

- Remove those distractions from your workspace.

9. The Strategy To Get Into Productive Mood Within Minutes

The Problem

Many times, we end up procrastinating because we are *"not in the mood"*. This usually happens due to overthinking. In our mind, we end up making the task more complex than it actually is. Afterwards, we cannot muster up enough energy to start doing it.

The Procrastination Solution

Once you figure out what needs to be done, follow through no matter what. Just start working. Do not worry about how much you can get done. Do not worry about the quality of your work. Your only focus should be on getting started. That's all. The hardest part is to begin. When you do that, it's easy to keep working.

This approach requires discipline. No matter how you are feeling, no matter what excuse your mind is giving you—"*Just leave it*," "*I am not in the mood*," "*I just want to see this episode on TV*," "*My friends are going out. I want to go too.*"

Don't listen to your excuses and start working. If you are REALLY not in the mood to do your work, you will have a 'bad' start. But instead of stopping, keep doing the work. In the beginning, your mind will resist it, but don't quit.

After a little while, your mind will stop resisting and accept the fact that work HAS to be done. From that point, you will be able to work with full effectiveness.

This technique helped me so much while writing this book. There were many days when I really didn't want to write. There was a lot of inner resistance. I would rather watch the ceiling fan spinning away than sit down and write. A big part of the problem was overthinking. I was worried that if I forced myself to write, the quality of my writing would turn out to be extremely bad. In my mind, I made a simple process of writing too complex to follow through.

But I forced myself to sit down and write. The first 10 minutes were the hardest. I couldn't think of what to write. I wasn't able to put sentences together. But I kept on writing. Usually, around the 10-minute mark, something clicks in the mind. The resistance goes away. Now I could think of what to write. I could now properly explain concepts, come up with examples, and add helpful tips to the content.

This approach is super effective, but it demands stern willpower at the beginning. So, it's not as easy as other strategies we have discussed till now. You need to exert control over your thoughts & emotions and get started. It requires effort but once it clicks, you'll find it easy to keep working for long hours.

"A difficult time can be readily endured if we retain the conviction that our existence holds a purpose – a cause to pursue, a person to love, a goal to achieve." – **John C. Maxwell,** American author, speaker, and pastor.

Summary

- Even when you are not in the mood, force yourself to start working.

- Once you begin, the mind tends to stop resisting the work. Thereby resulting in increased productivity.

10. The Community Advantage

The Problem

If you tend to do most of your work by yourself, it feels like you against the world. You feel lonely. You feel overwhelmed. It gets harder and harder to motivate yourself.

Sometimes, loneliness is the reason behind your procrastination habit. Maybe you are tired of facing challenges alone. Maybe you need support and guidance. It is understandable. As social creatures, we perform better when we are a part of a group working towards a singular objective.

The Procrastination Solution

An interesting fact about human relationships is that people who stick together are not necessarily those who share the same traits or character make-up, but those who share and collectively fight the same problems. Furthermore, you find it more helpful in finding someone who has this problem and is passionate about and committed to solving it than going it all alone.

One of the greatest advantages of humanity is working collaboratively to achieve a common goal. We are hardwired to work together. In research done at Stanford, it was found that when we work together with other people, it increases our motivation, *even when we are physically apart.*

In an article in *Journal of Experimental psychology,* Gregory Walton and Priyanka Carr wrote, "*While keeping other factors constant, participants exposed to cues of working together showed more persistence, enjoyed the activity more, and even performed better on the task.*" When we work together with others on a common problem, it can increase our intrinsic motivation.

Throughout human history, we have always responded to a cause that is bigger than ourselves. Every outstanding achievement we have ever had was as a result of people working collaboratively to attain a specific objective.

When you join a community that is working towards a common end, the surge of motivation boost is undeniably powerful. Here's an analogy that I like. Scattered rays of light don't have much power. When you put your hand through them, it's harmless. But when combined and focused in a single direction, they turn into a laser that can melt steel.

Putting It Into Action

First, you will need to find a community of people that have similar goals to yours. It can be anything from a nearby local club to an online group.

Usually, local groups don't have a fee to join. A desire to join is usually enough. Some groups do charge a small fee for exclusive member features. Whether you need those exclusive member benefits is up to you. So it's a good idea to gather some information from the other group members before going for exclusive membership. Overall, joining a local community is a good choice if you prefer in-person meetings.

Online communities are what I personally like and recommend to most people. They are easy to find no matter where you are located. All you need to do is run a google search, and you will get several results instantly. Just type in – "your goal" followed by "groups."

For example, if you want to join a community where people focus on improving their productivity; then search "productivity groups." You'll instantly get several productivity-oriented groups in the search results. Take your pick. It is as simple as that.

Being a part of a community and sharing a common goal provides you with moral support, a sense of belonging, new solutions to problems, and healthy competition. It gives you the motivation to push further and harder than you could alone.

We have been living in communities from the start of human evolution and will continue to form communities in the future. It's time for you to use it for your benefit.

> "Alone we can do so little; together we can do so much." – **Helen Keller**, American author, activist, and lecturer.

Summary

- Join a community that has similar goals to your own goals.

- It can increase your intrinsic motivation and help in overcoming procrastination.

11. Why Is Peer-to-Peer Accountability A Game Changer

The Problem

As discussed previously, when you work alone, there is no one to hold you accountable if you procrastinate. Being part of a community is an excellent strategy to handle that situation. But what if you don't want to join a community for any reason? Maybe you can't find the right community, or maybe you're shy. What would you do in that case? Fortunately, there are other options. An excellent one is – having an accountability partner.

The Procrastination Solution

Procrastinating is common when you're working on a goal yourself, but when you have to check-in with another person, it is almost embarrassing to postpone. An accountability partner is likely to keep you on track and working each day towards your goal.

Benefits of an Accountability Partner

1. When you have someone frequently checking on your progress, you'll be much more likely to meet your goals daily. It will nearly become impossible to put off tasks that you need to finish today because at the end of the day, you'll need to check-in with your accountability partner.

2. Receiving support from somebody else gives you the motivation to pursue your goals. Sometimes, just having someone to speak with; can really motivate you to keep going once you hit a roadblock. Talk the matter through together with your accountability partner, and you'll renew your energy.

3. An accountability partner will keep you focused on your goal and the steps you need to take to gain that achievement. You want a strong person because they will ensure that you do not give up or slack in meeting your benchmarks and ultimate goal. They will remind you why you're doing it in the first place.

4. When working on your own, sometimes it's easier to give up than make adjustments. Having an accountability partner means that you can talk things through and come to a logical decision which is not based on fear, doubt, or laziness.

How to Select an Accountability Partner?

Having an accountability partner can be a game-changer. But you have to be careful about whom you choose. Here are a few things to keep in mind while selecting an accountability partner.

1. Genuine Interest

Your accountability partner should be someone that has a genuine interest in your success. They should really want to see you do well. They should ask you questions about your progress and celebrate when you achieve a milestone.

2. Brutally Honest

Your partner must be someone who will call you on things if you're not keeping your commitments. Brutal honesty is required from them. They shouldn't ignore your mistakes and allow you to slack off because they don't want you to feel bad. The role of an accountability partner is to tell you exactly what you need to hear. A tough-love approach is ideal.

3. Positivity

Pick a person with a positive demeanor. Your outlook affects every area of your life.

When you've finished a conversation with your accountability partner, you ought to feel uplifted and encouraged. Obviously, not everyone is often positive all the time. But if you notice that most of your conversations are negative, then it may be time for a change.

4. Trust

Pick someone you trust. A significant part of being accountability partners is sharing your hopes & dreams. That's why you need to find someone that you trust and that believes in you. You want to be completely sure that you both have a shared vision.

5. Mutual support

A partnership goes both ways. While you want to find someone that will support you, it's wiser to choose a partner that you believe in and are willing to support as well. Mutual support would make your partnership last a long time.

> *"Accountability is essential for personal growth. How can you improve if you are never wrong? If you don't admit a mistake and take responsibility for it, you're bound to make the same one again."* – **Pat Summitt**, American women's basketball coach with 1098 career wins.

Summary

• When you're working by yourself, there is no one to hold you accountable if you procrastinate.

• Having an accountability partner is likely to keep you working each day towards your goal.

12. What Is Professional Expertise And Why It Matters

The Problem

As we previously discussed, being part of a community and having an accountability partner are excellent ways to ensure that you stay on track and be productive. But what happens if you need more guidance? Maybe you want to cut to the absolute best option available for tapping into new levels of productivity and success?

The Procrastination Solution

If you want the absolute best alternative, then I would recommend getting a mentor. In today's distraction-filled world, having a mentor could be one of the deciding factors to increase your productivity. You may be willing to take action but perhaps feel like something is holding you back. A mentor can pinpoint the exact issue and guide you through it.

A mentor has been through the journey that you are on. They have been there and done that. They know what to expect and can provide valuable guidance, insights, knowledge, and support throughout the way. Many of the most successful people in history had mentors. Here are some of the most famous mentoring relationships:

- Steve Jobs was a mentor to Mark Zuckerberg.

- Steven Spielberg was a mentor to J.J. Abrams.

- Maya Angelou was a mentor to Oprah Winfrey.

- Aristotle was a mentor to Alexander the Great.

"I think mentors are important, and I don't think anybody makes it in the world without some form of mentorship." – **Oprah Winfrey**, American talk show host, author, philanthropist.

Very few people will understand what you are going through. That's one of the biggest benefits of having a mentor. They have already achieved the goal that you are pursuing. They know the battlefield. They are familiar with the challenges and opportunities. They have found solutions to the problems and can help to guide you through them.

A mentor will analyze your character and in turn familiarize you with your strengths and weaknesses. They will tell you what you are doing right and what you need to learn. They will point you in the right direction, saving you a lot of time and effort.

You can count on your mentor to give you honest feedback. They will tell you about the things, as they really stand, instead of worrying about how you would feel. While they care about you and love to see you happy, they won't hold back the truth even if it upsets you a little. You will always receive an honest response which can be immensely helpful for your growth.

How to Find a Mentor?

Finding a mentor is a challenge in itself. Here's a four-step process for maximizing your chances of finding one:

1. Evaluate your goals: Think about the goals you want to achieve and what it will take to achieve them. Clarity is power. The clearer you are about your goals, the better it is. Because when you know what you want, you'll be able to determine what kind of mentor you need. You'll be looking for those traits in potential mentors.

2. Start the search: Once the goals are decided, you have so many options to begin your search for a mentor. Start with your social circle. Do any of your friends and family know someone that fits the role? If not, then search your workplace for connections. Some other options include entrepreneurial meetups, non-profit organizations, seminars, social events. As the last option, you can search online for mentors who will fit your requirements.

There are various social media groups and websites dedicated to connecting you with potential mentors. Be careful as some may be scams. That is why many people don't prefer online mentoring. It can work, however. I have seen people find great mentors online. It is certainly possible, but someone in your immediate connection or at least in your city is preferred.

3. Be authentic: Once you find someone, try to meet them in person. Sending emails doesn't work as well. Once you meet them, tell them about your goals. Be real. Many times, your authenticity will be the deciding factor in whether they accept your request or not.

4. Show your intentions clearly: Furthermore, tell them why you chose them as a potential mentor. How do you think they could help you achieve your goals, AND what can you do for them in return? That's correct. You have to find some way to give across value in return. It may be monetary or something else. For instance, maybe to do something for them for free? Lend a helping hand. Connect them to someone you know. There are so many ways to give value in return. You just have to know what they need. You can find their needs by doing some background research beforehand, or you could just ask them politely. Even if they don't need anything, they would appreciate the gesture, increasing the chances that they'd accept your request.

"One of the greatest values of mentors is the ability to see ahead what others cannot see and to help them navigate a course to their destination." — **John C. Maxwell**, author, and speaker.

Summary

- Being productive can be challenging if you mostly work alone.

- Mentors provide valuable guidance, insights, knowledge, and support throughout the way.

- Many of the most successful people in history have had mentors.

- Use the four-step process to maximize your chances of finding a mentor.

13. The "First 5-Minutes" Technique

The Problem

Most of the tasks we have to complete are not difficult to do. We are perfectly capable of doing them. However, we still procrastinate on them for various reasons. Maybe we find a task too boring, or maybe we are overwhelmed with the workload. For example, a student may procrastinate about doing a home assignment because they find the subject too boring, or an employee avoids a new project because they have a lot of things to do. Whatever may be the reason, we start making excuses to do it later.

The Procrastination Solution

The first 5-minutes technique is a wonderful tool to overcome procrastination and begin taking action. If there is a task you have to do but for some reason, you really don't feel like doing it, tell yourself that you'll only do it for five minutes. Once you start doing it, you will gain momentum and will not want to stop before finishing it.

Why It Works?

According to psychology studies, the human mind is terrible at predicting how we would feel after a future event. It's very inaccurate at predicting how we will feel after finishing a task. Often, we procrastinate because we think doing the task will be a painful experience.

Link to study:
https://www.ncbi.nlm.nih.gov/pmc/articles/PMC2666705/

But when we commit to working for only five minutes and get started, we realize that it's not as bad as we thought. Once we engage with the task, all our worries and resistance disappear. We are filled with positive feelings of accomplishing an important task and are likely to continue till it is done.

<u>Note</u> - It's important that you tell yourself that you only need to do the work for five minutes. After five minutes, if you don't want to continue, it's fine. There should be no guilt for leaving it unfinished. The whole point of this technique is to reduce stress and make working on the task as effortless as possible. If you *force* yourself to continue past five minutes, it may create resistance. You are better off taking a break and starting again later. You'll have much better chances of getting the work done.

*"Courage is not having the strength to go on; it is **going on** when you don't have the strength."* – **Theodore Roosevelt**, 26th President of the United States.

Summary

- If you are having trouble starting, do the work for only five minutes.

- Once you start doing it, you will gain momentum and would keep working until it's done.

14. The Truth Behind Preparation. Is It Worth The Effort

James's story

A client of mine, James, wanted to lose weight. He went ahead and googled *"how to lose weight."* He came across a new dieting method called the *Keto diet*. After reading its benefits and the fantastic success stories, he got pumped up and decided to begin his new keto diet first thing - tomorrow morning.

So let's fast forward to the next morning. After coming back from an hour-long walk, he went straight to the kitchen. He kept reminding himself, *"okay. 10% carbohydrates, and 90% protein & fats. It seems easy enough."*

After fumbling for 15 minutes in the fridge and kitchen drawers, he found some ingredients to make a keto breakfast. He didn't know how to prepare it so he looked online for recipes. It took him half an hour to prepare his breakfast.

He had to put in a similar effort to prepare lunch and dinner.

"So far so good."

The next morning, he was not as enthusiastic about making keto breakfast. *"It's not as easy as I thought."* But he forced himself to prepare the breakfast, lunch, and dinner according to keto diet. In the end, he was exhausted.

Again, the next morning came. He thought, *"oh no! Do I have to make all that today too? I am really not in the mood right now. I'll do it tomorrow."*

And tomorrow it was exactly the same. Following Keto diet was too difficult for him. It was much easier to fall back to his normal diet - which he did.

After one year, he was having a coaching call with me. After hearing his story, I realized he needed help in preparation. I recommended him to consult a dietician. He went to a dietician and told her his previous experience. The dietician advised him on how to prepare everything BEFORE starting a keto diet.

James started again. This time, he brought some good keto-recipe books. Then, he planned out keto meals for the entire week. After that, he went to the supermarket and brought all the ingredients needed for the whole week. Everything was put in the kitchen. All the ingredients were in place. The recipe books were right at the kitchen table.

The very next morning, he had to spend less than 10 minutes to prepare a keto breakfast. This time, it really was easy.

Later, he cooked several keto meals and put them in the fridge. All it took was 2 minutes in the oven to be ready to eat. He followed the diet for two months and lost ten pounds.

This is the power of being *well-prepared*.

James went from quitting the diet in two days, to losing ten pounds in two months. But, it all came down to preparation.

Being prepared is an extraordinary tool to beat procrastination and save time. Realization of any goal requires you to face many challenges. And if you are not prepared, then you could end up facing multiple problems at once.

You may get overwhelmed. It may lead to procrastination or even quitting. So, prepare in advance. I love the quote, *"being *well prepared is like winning half the battle."* Being prepared is a must.

Try to collect information, gather items, and ready your team beforehand. So later when you come across challenges, you're better equipped to deal with it.

Note about preparation – As mentioned in earlier strategies, some people take it *too far*. They spend all of their time preparing and forget to take action. While preparation is recommended, you should not get overwhelmed by it. When you ask someone why they are not starting, you'll get replies like, *"I will start when I figure everything out."*

Let me be the one to tell you that you won't figure everything out through preparation. Action is equally or more important. There is a reason why great achievers have always said, *"experience is the best teacher."*

Experience - through taking action - will provide the most valuable lessons you'll learn in life. So don't hold yourself back. Embrace action. Start doing the work.

Preparation is important but it cannot take place of action. That is why I recommend being *reasonably* prepared - which means being prepared enough to know the basics - and then just start taking action. This should help in maintaining a balance between preparation and action, which is important as tilting too much on either side should be avoided.

"No man ever reached to excellence in any one art or profession without having passed through the slow and painful process of study and preparation." – **Horace, Ancient Roman Poet.**

Summary

- Be prepared before starting a task.

- Familiarize yourself with the basics and start taking action.

- You'll learn more as you take action.

15. Unreliability Of Passion and Emotions

The Problem

One big excuse that procrastinators grapple with and which they use frequently as a reason for them not getting to work - is that they feel the time is not right or that they've not got their motivation going yet. But all of these may best be termed as implausible excuses.

The Procrastination Solution

If you wait till you get the right ignition or till the motivation comes over you, or till the timing becomes "right," you will seldom get anything done. Several stories that achievers have told us is that these people are devoid of emotions and feelings, at least when doing their work.

Most of us are passionate about different things: acting/theatre, music, sports, finance, etc. We might attend events or read stories about those that have succeeded in these areas. It gives us that motivation, that ignition, that 'vibe.' But we just never start. Why? Ignition, motivation, inspiration, vibe, and other similar emotions are driven by hormones that are secreted and which manifest at different times.

But to succeed at things we have interest in, the work has to be put in at all times, irrespective of 'when the vibe comes.' It has been reported that those who excel in fields such as literature and arts and other creative works of life that need 'vibe' or 'inspiration' don't work based on those ephemeral and unstable emotions.

They just do it.

What Science Says?

New research conducted by Andrea Bonezzi, an assistant marketing professor at Stern School of Business, suggested that people's motivation can drop halfway through their journey to achieve a predetermined goal.

In the study titled "Stuck in the Middle: The Psychophysics of Goal Pursuit," Bonezzi debunked the myth that motivation increases as we reach closer to the end goal. People's motivation can be higher when they are starting out and when about to reach their goal. The middle part of the journey is where motivation at its lowest. Because both – the start and the end – seem distant. That's what usually causes the "stuck in the middle" phenomenon.

Let's look at an example. Suppose a book has thirty chapters. A student preparing for tests can usually breeze through the book's first ten chapters due to higher initial motivation. It's also easier for them to finish the last ten because they are near the finish line. The hardest part is the mid-portion of the book – the ten chapters in the middle. Because both – the start and the end – seem far away, it gives the illusion that finishing one chapter doesn't seem to be making any difference.

That is why we cannot depend on emotions like motivation. It will not always be with you. Sooner or later, you'd have to continue the work regardless of how you feel.

Mason Currey reports in "Daily Rituals: How Artists Work" that W. H. Auden, the award-winning poet, once stated that: *"A modern stoic knows that the surest way to discipline passion is to discipline time; decide what you would like or need to do during the day, then always roll in the hay at precisely the same moment a day, and keenness will give you no trouble."*

If you wait for vibe or passion all the time, then think about how great achievers go about it. For instance, Cristiano Ronaldo, Lionel Messi, and other great sportspeople have to play weekly or even bi-weekly outside of their compulsory training. If they wait for motivation or passion, then they won't get anything done. Because it can never be said that they always have the vibe every day!

Top entrepreneurs like Elon Musk, Jeff Bezos, Richard Branson do not depend on motivation because it is simply not enough to carry them throughout the workday. They work regardless of how they feel.

Don't let your emotions decide your schedule. The most important thing is that you get to the work anyway. Refer to chapters 4, 9, and 13 for strategies to get started without depending on motivation.

> *"When something is important enough, you do it even if the odds are not in your favor."* – **Elon Musk**, Entrepreneur, designer, engineer.

Summary

- Emotions like motivation, passion, and vibe are unpredictable.

- Try to develop a habit of doing work irrespective of how you feel.

16. The Transformative Power Of "Consequence" Exercise

The Problem

Have you noticed that you have become stagnant career-wise because you just don't seem to have the motivation and self-discipline to search for new opportunities consistently? Have you ever decided to wake up early but cannot help but sleep in quite often? Do you find it hard to follow any fitness program just because of your soft spot for desserts?

The Procrastination Solution

One of the qualities of action-takers is to access the long and short-term consequences of their work. The value of the work is determined by how it can impact your future. This evaluation is the determiner of our next step.

In the 1960s, psychologist Walter Mischel and his colleagues conducted one of the most famous experiments in history called the "Marshmallow Test." The researchers gave marshmallows to a group of preschool children. Each child was given one marshmallow and was told to ring the bell if they want to eat their marshmallow. But if they could resist eating the marshmallow for 15 minutes, they would be given a second one as a reward. Some kids ate the first marshmallow while some decided to wait.

Years later, Walter and his team reconnected with the kids (who had grown up now) to see how are they doing in life. It was found that the kids who decided to wait for the second one fared better in life than others who had eaten immediately.

This experiment proves how long-term thinking is related to becoming happier and more successful in life. The way you value time is a huge predictor of your choices and actions. People who realize the significance of time generally make better decisions than people who don't.

Highly productive people are constantly thinking about the future. Their daily schedule is a reflection of their future-oriented thinking.

The Consequences Exercise

Here's a powerful exercise to develop a future-oriented mindset.

First, you have to get clear about what you want to achieve. It is the intensity of your desire for the goal that determines where it gets placed on your to-do list. The more we value something, the more willing we are to act on it.

If you truly care about your goal, you should be afraid of not achieving it. You should be afraid of the negative consequences of not taking action. You should be afraid of losing it forever.

It is commonly advised that we should think positively, but we are looking to do the opposite. We want to capitalize on the fear of failure. We want to use fear as fuel for taking action. And it works like a charm. Here's the next step.

Once you decide what you want, ask yourself the following questions:

- How would my life look in the future if I don't take action now?

- If I don't take action, how would my life be after 5 years?

- How would my life be after 10 years?

- How would my life be after 20 years?

Take a notebook and write down every possible negative consequence in *detail*. Go deep. All these scenarios should be quite upsetting, to say the least. Keep writing till you get to a point where you can't take it anymore. You just can't imagine living a life like that.

The point of this exercise is to provide a close-up look at the future consequences of not taking action. It is to intimate you with the life waiting for you if you don't act now. You will become crystal clear about the importance of your goals and why you shouldn't waste a single second procrastinating.

This exercise can be terrifying and eye-opening at the same time. It was a revelation for me when I first found out about it. I still practice it to this day, at least once or twice a month, to remind myself why I do what I do.

If you don't think about the future in detail and are struggling with procrastination, give this exercise a try. I love it as do many of my clients. It is simple, easy, and super effective!

> *"If you do not think about the future, you cannot have one."* –
> **John Galsworthy**, English novelist, and playwright.

Summary

- A common cause of procrastination is a lack of clarity.

- Getting familiar with what you want is the first step towards being productive.

- Use the consequences exercise to understand the dreadful ramifications of inaction.

17. The Unpleasant Alternative

The Problem

Do you ever wonder why you sometimes procrastinate on important tasks and choose to do other activities that are a complete waste of time? For example, why does a person decides to watch a movie when they have a project needing their immediate attention?

This is a very common phenomenon that everybody experiences from time to time. Let's take a look at the reason behind it.

The Procrastination Solution

Often, you hesitate to get started because (1) the work is boring (2) there are better, more fun alternatives like hanging out with friends, watching TV, surfing the net, and so on.

That almost always results in you choosing the fun activity over work. While it makes sense on the surface, there is a deeper psychological reason for it.

Austrian neurologist Sigmund Freud, who is known as the founder of psychoanalysis, proposed the principle of *pain* and *pleasure*. According to Freud, all humans take actions to move away from pain and move towards pleasure. It is the basis of all decisions that we make. For instance, going up to someone you find attractive and introducing yourself can lead to possible rejection, which is painful, so many people hesitate to do that.

The pain of rejection outweighs the potential pleasure of meeting someone new. Compare that to eating a piece of chocolate cake, which is a source of pleasure. Do you need a lot of convincing to pick up a slice? Probably not! The pleasure outweighs the potential health issues of eating sugar-rich food.

This is true for all the decisions we make in life. We always choose to increase pleasure or decrease pain and it makes sense. We want to feel good. We try to avoid feeling bad. The procrastination problem arises when you get more pleasure from unproductive activities than your work.

When you get more pleasure from watching TV than working on a task, the mind instinctively chooses to watch TV. At this point, the principle of pain and pleasure is working against us.

So, what can we do here? Is there a way to make pain & pleasure help us instead?

Using Pain and Pleasure to Boost Productivity

Here's an effective approach - set yourself a penalty for not taking action.

Okay. This might sound extreme, but having a slightly painful 'consequence' for procrastinating is simply enough motivation to urge things done.

For instance, maybe you've postponed updating your resume despite the urgent need. Here's something you can do. Have your friend send it out *incomplete* to your three favorite companies if you don't finish it today. It will be so embarrassing that you'll make sure to update your resume today.

In my experience, and studies confirm, that punishment can be a powerful source of motivation. In fact, many experts consider pain to be a more powerful motivating factor than pleasure. Let's look at an example. Suppose you have 5000 dollars and you decide to spend it in a casino. But there's a catch. You have a 50% chance to earn another 5000 dollars and a 50% chance to lose 5000 that you currently have. Would you take that chance?

For most people, the answer would be 'no.' Because avoiding the pain of losing 5000 dollars is more motivating than receiving an extra 5000. That's how we generally think — avoiding pain triumphs over getting pleasure most of the time.

So, punishment works. Period! But how do we apply it to our work life?

Here's a punishment strategy especially designed for overcoming procrastination: **not indulging in any alternate fun activities**.

Here's how it works. When you don't take action, as a punishment, you will not do any fun activities like watching TV, browsing social media, eating pizza, drinking alcohol, and similar things. You abstain from all of the fun alternatives. The only thing you are allowed to "do" is to just sit and do nothing.

The absence of fun alternatives will make you bored out of your mind. It will make you think about doing the work because if there is one thing we hate more than doing work... It's to do nothing at all. Imagine sitting on your chair and staring at the wall.

Punishing yourself like this will make you re-think your decisions. You'll realize that it is no use procrastinating. The alternative is even worse. Remember what we discussed about pain and pleasure earlier. Subconsciously, you would start to associate procrastination with extreme boredom (pain).

Slowly, doing work may start looking like a superior choice. It is comparatively more engaging than sitting around doing nothing. Just sitting will bore you out of your mind. The pain of boredom will make taking action look far more interesting.

See what we have done here? We associated pain with procrastination and pleasure with doing work. When you do this, you won't have to force yourself to work. You'd want to get up and start working.

Use pain and pleasure to your advantage, and you'd never have to worry about procrastination. When you see how much worse the alternative is, you will gladly choose to work every time, which is exactly what we want.

Please do not underestimate this technique. It has worked wonders for many of my clients, and I sincerely believe it will benefit you as well. Apply it. It might end up saving you a lot of time and frustration while taking your productivity to the next level.

> *"The secret of success is learning how to use pain and pleasure instead of having pain and pleasure use you. If you do that, you're in control of your life. If you don't, life controls you."* –
> **Tony Robbins**, American author, coach, speaker, and philanthropist.

Summary

- People's primary motivation is to move away from pain and move towards pleasure.

- Procrastination occurs when you get more pleasure from non-productive activities than doing the work.

- A very effective solution is to set a penalty for not taking action. It will associate pain with inaction and pleasure with work.

- Do this correctly, and you won't ever have to force yourself to work. You'd want to get up and take action.

18. The Trap Of Perfectionism

The Problem

Many times, we hesitate to get started because we have set the bar too high.

For instance, Joe joined a yoga class. In his enthusiasm, he has decided that he will go to the class 6 days a week. But Joe did not account for the fact that he has to attend college lectures during the day and work at a part-time job in the evening. His schedule is already quite hectic, even before adding the "6-days-a-week" commitment into the mix.

After the first week, he started feeling exhausted and tired from his jam-packed schedule. Not being able to cope up with the pressure, he decided to quit the yoga class altogether. His friends advised him not to stop completely. Instead, he should go to the yoga class three times a week. That would ease out his schedule and give him more time to relax.

But Joe believes he has to go six days a week. Otherwise, it's not worth his time. It's either six days a week or none at all.

Joe has set the standard too high. It's a bar that he cannot meet on a consistent basis. Thus, anything lower is just not acceptable to him. So he ends up quitting.

Joe's high standards set him up for failure and procrastination. As a beginner, it's quite tempting to set the bar too high. That almost always leads to procrastination, as very high standards make it difficult to get started and be consistent.

In a multi-generational study conducted from 1989 to 2016, researchers Thomas Curran and Andrew Hill found a significant increase in perfectionism among recent undergraduates of the USA, UK, and Canada. With the increasing popularity of social media, our society is slowly being pushed toward perfectionism.

It is neither good for productivity nor your health. A lot of studies have found perfectionism to be associated with several mental and physical problems. Here are a few problems with links to studies:

In a report published in 2005, researchers Murray W. Enns & Brian J. Cox found a strong association between perfectionism and depression. A 2014 study conducted by Alicia Handley, Sarah Egan, Robert Kane, & Clare Rees found an association between perfectionism and generalized anxiety disorder.

Perfectionism is not a standard. It's an obstacle. We need to let it go.

The Procrastination Solution

The key is to lower our expectations at the beginning. If Joe had decided to go to the gym three days a week instead of six, he wouldn't have quit. Lowering our expectations make it much easier to get started. It allows us to be consistent and, thus, feel like a success. We start taking more action and get even better results, creating an upward spiral of productivity and confidence.

Top 8 Signs That You May Be a Perfectionist:

1. You set lofty goals even at the beginning stage.
2. You prefer the "all-or-nothing" approach.
3. You are never satisfied with your performance.
4. You try very hard to get things right the first time.
5. Anything less than perfect feels like a failure.
6. You are obsessed with past mistakes.
7. You often fail to meet deadlines.

8. You cannot accept being the second-best.

If you can identify with a few of these signs, then you may be a perfectionist. While this is not always a bad thing, it can lead to procrastination issues. The solution is to reduce the expectations a little. It will make it easier to get started.

Don't strive to be perfect in an imperfect world. You'll never be satisfied with your work. Instead, aim for being *"better-than-yesterday."*

On that note, it's important to mention that you're not limited in any way. Once you've gained some experience, you can always raise the standard. It's a natural progression. Lowering the bar allows you to overcome the initial resistance. Once you gain momentum, you'll probably feel like you can do more and end up raising the standard.

> *"Perfectionism is a dangerous state of mind in an imperfect world"* – **Robert Hillyer**, American poet.

Summary

- Try not to set very high expectations, especially at the beginning.

- Lowering the bar makes it easier to overcome procrastination.

- Once you've gained some experience, you can always raise the standard. It's a natural progression.

19. Focus On "What" Instead Of "How"

The Problem

Another factor that stops us from getting started is we don't know *how* to accomplish a task. This is especially true for long-term projects or goals.

You are afraid that you don't know *how* you will achieve your goal. You have no clue, and there's no clear path visible at *this* moment. What should we do in this situation?

The Procrastination Solution

Don't let *'how'* stop you. You don't need to know *how* you will achieve your goals right now. Just knowing *what* you want is enough! You'll figure out how to do it later... when you start taking action. According to Dr. Maxwell Maltz, the human mind is the world's greatest problem-solving system. It will figure out the *'how'*.

Resource: For a psychological discussion about our brain's exceptional problem-solving skills, read *Psycho-Cybernetics* by Dr. Maxwell Maltz.

In the beginning, focus on being clear about what you want. Do not think about how you will achieve it. I, myself, didn't know this when I started. I doubted if I could ever figure out a way to achieve some of my goals. They were outside my reality. But I kept on moving forward with whatever information I had at the time.

Later, I was quite surprised by the fact that I *could* figure it out. All of a sudden, solutions would pop up, or I would meet someone who helped to move me closer to my destination. I couldn't believe it at first. I thought it was pure luck. But after going through this cycle several times, I firmly believe that our minds are quite capable of finding a solution to any problem we might face. It really is a wonderful gift.

For instance, Thomas Edison had failed 10,000 times before he finally invented the light bulb. He said those mistakes and failures taught him lessons that helped him finally create the light bulb.

When he started out, he didn't know how he was going to make a light bulb. He started with whatever he knew and 'figured-it-out' later.

You must *trust* the process. Have faith that the path will become clear when you decide *where* you want to go. If you can see your destination, you can find a path to it.

> *"Whatever we plant in our subconscious mind, and nourish it with repetition and emotion, will one day become a reality."* - **Earl Nightingale**, motivational speaker, author.

Believe in yourself and your dreams. Because people who don't, tend to give up even before they take their first step. If you read autobiographies of renowned leaders, you will find they didn't know *how* they would achieve their goals initially. But they had trust and kept going. The *'how'* became apparent along the way.

That is the way every great achiever obtains success. Let's look at another example.

Walt Disney dreamed of a wonderful place where people could go and forget all their worries. He had an amazing vision, but no money.

To fund Disneyland, he approached ten banks, but they turned down his application. He approached another ten banks, and they turned him down too. After many other rejections, most people would have quit. But he didn't.

He tried different approaches, speeches, and presentations. Finally, one bank was able to see his vision and agreed to fund Disneyland, but it took Walt Disney 300 rejections to get it done! He was rejected by 300 banks before he got just one bank to agree.

That is trust. He had no idea how he was going to arrange funds, but he kept going, and most importantly, didn't give up when times were hard. He had a firm belief that he was going to make it. Disneyland wasn't just his dream; it was a dream for the world.

And now Disneyland is a reality.

It stands there as a beacon of joy and happiness for the whole world because the man who envisioned it didn't quit.

You must do the same. Take the first step. Your journey will show you the path. Have faith in the process.

> *"Life is never made unbearable by circumstances, but only by lack of meaning and purpose."* – **Viktor Frankl**, Austrian neurologist, author, and Holocaust survivor.

Summary

- Become crystal clear about what you want.

- Don't be afraid of how will you do it.

- Start taking action anyway. Keep going. You'll figure out how along the way.

20. The Principle Of Calculated Influence

The Problem

Many times, procrastination is a behavior you acquire from the people around you.

Attitude is highly contagious. We all have a few *excuse-makers* in our life. It's best to maintain your distance if you are looking to improve your productivity.

Here's a real story about how others affect your mindset. One of my friends introduced me to Luke. At first, I liked him. But later, when I started hanging out with him, I realized he was always complaining about everything. He could find fault in everything and everyone. No matter how I tried to be positive around him, his strong negative outlook overwhelmed me every time.

Soon 'I' started pointing out faults in things, which I don't normally do. My other friends began telling me that I was changing. I was not as positive and upbeat as before. At that time, I realized how strongly people influence each other. I minimized my interactions with Luke. And it was the biggest thing that helped me get back to feeling positive and upbeat.

The Procrastination Solution

Surrounding yourself with productive people is a great way to overcome the procrastination habit.

Hang out with people who are taking action consistently. Watch how they talk, what they do, how they think. Expose yourself to productive people as much as possible.

> *"Associate yourself with people of good quality, for it is better to be alone than in bad company"* **- Booker T. Washington,** American educator, author, and advisor to Presidents of the United States.

It is a psychological fact that we become a combination of five people with whom we spend most of our time. According to research by Dr. David McClelland of Harvard, the people you associate with determine as much as 95 percent of your success or failure in life.

We subconsciously absorb the thinking of the other person, whether it is positive or negative. That's the way our brains are wired. Be around successful, positive, action-oriented people, and your mind will start adopting their behavior automatically.

What to Do if You Can't Find Productive People Around You?

Don't be discouraged if you can't find productive people to hang out with. I discovered that, positive well-written books, audio, video programs, etc., all count towards changing your mind to be productive. It's not only about the surrounding people. It's about the top five "influences" that affect you on a daily basis.

Reading a book by someone who is massively productive *will* influence your mind to think like them. As you continually read, watch or listen to top individuals, you will gradually begin to adopt their mindset and behaviors, which would be *really* helpful if you can't find people like that in your social circle.

One of the biggest benefits of having an action-oriented mindset is that it changes your focus from "surviving" to "thriving." Have you noticed people who are just coping through life? Their whole motivation is to "get by." For them, having just enough to survive is fine.

With the action-oriented mindset, you will see situations and people differently. Your focus will be on what's good and what's possible. There will be higher energy inside you, which other people will notice. You will have more passion and zest for life. You'll see challenges and difficulties merely as a stepping stone to success.

"Be the one thing you think you cannot do. Fail at it. Try again. Do better the second time. The only people who don't tumble at the high wire are those who never mount the high wire" **- Oprah Winfrey,** American talk show host and actress.

Summary

● Being in the company of productive people is a proven way to overcome the procrastination habit.

● Good books, audiobooks, and videos also help in shifting your mindset.

21. The Secret To Unleashing Your Inner Drive

The Problem

One of the most common causes of the procrastination habit is not knowing your reasons for doing work. A person, who is not clear about what they want, is like a leaf blowing in the wind, constantly changing directions without a set path.

Why do you want to take action? What are you looking to get from it? What is it that you actually want? People who don't know the purpose behind their work struggle with motivation issues. They feel lost, bored, and succumb easily to distractions.

So the question arises; how do we find our *reasons* and use them to overcome procrastination?

The Procrastination Solution

The first thing is to get a pen & paper and ask yourself these questions:

- Why am I doing the work?

- What will it allow me to do or feel?

- What positive changes will it bring?

- How will the realization of my goals help me and others?

Write down everything that comes to mind. These are the reasons which form the "why" you want to acquire your goals. Create a list.

These reasons could be financial, physical, spiritual, or mental. Whatever they might be, if they make you feel motivated, add them to your list. Make sure the reasons are authentic, which means they are your personal reasons. Whenever you think about them, you will feel inspired.

The higher the number of reasons in your list - the better. More than any particular reason, it's the cumulative impact of this list that will boost your motivation to a higher level. And best of all, it is available to you all the time. You can access it at any moment.

I recommend reviewing this list three times a day. It will only take a minute or so. When repeated over a period of time, it will get deeply imprinted in your mind, giving clarity to your motives behind the work. You'll find yourself a lot more focused and motivated.

Note #1. Use a pen and paper. Some people ask why this has to be a 'written' list. Why can't they just have these in mind?

Using the old-fashioned pen and paper for this list is one of the most important tips that I can give you. Studies have proven that using pen and paper for writing provides amazing psychological and productivity benefits. Writing by hand is superior to typing on a computer or mobile phone. It improves memory, encourages deeper thinking and reflection, and builds new neural connections in the brain.

Link to study:
https://journals.sagepub.com/doi/abs/10.1177/0956797614524581

Note #2. Positive statements. Another important point is to make sure your reasons are positive, not negative. For example, "*I will be fully financially independent when I achieve my goal*" is a positive reason. Don't write it as "*I will be able to pay my bills and move out of this horrible situation.*"

The first reason is written in a positive tone and feels much more uplifting and powerful. The second makes you focus on the negative, even if its overall meaning is positive. According to Neuro-Linguistic Programming (NLP), our brains do not process negative commands. For example:

"Don't think about a pink elephant."

While reading the above statement, did you imagine a pink-colored elephant? But the command was to not think about a pink elephant. Did you see that? Our brain doesn't process negative commands like 'no' or 'do not' or 'cannot.'

Whenever you say to yourself, *"I do not want more debt."* Your brain doesn't process the word – do not. It hears, *"I want more debt."*

And according to neuroscience, what you repeatedly say to yourself is deeply imprinted in the brain. That is the reason why you should always use positive statements when talking to yourself. You don't want to store negative thoughts in the brain by accident. Make sure your reasons are written in the positive, which will make you focus on the positive effects of achieving your goals.

"The two most important days in your life are; the day you were born, and the day you find out why" – **Mark Twain**, American write, entrepreneur, humorist.

Summary

- Ask yourself, *"why am I doing the work?"*

- Create a list of the reasons.

- Review this list at least three times a day.

22. The "Catch & Redirect" Technique

The Problem

You know in your heart, that you procrastinate; that's why you are reading this book. Acknowledging that you have an issue at hand is the first - albeit the most difficult step - in overcoming procrastination and that is commendable. However, as has already been said, that is only the first step. What is next?

The Procrastination Solution

The next is as simple and as complicated as anything. It is to start. At its core, the best way to get disciplined or to defeat procrastination is to just begin. Our favorite sportswear manufacturer, Nike, puts it this way, *"JUST DO IT."*

So far, we have reiterated this repeatedly - the most difficult thing to do is to start. For instance, finishing up or completing a project is not half as difficult as starting the project in the first place. Pay close attention to your actions and catch yourself while procrastinating. Now that you are aware, *"oh, I've been procrastinating so far,"* pick up your gear and get to work. If you are not able to "just start," use the techniques you learn in this book. They will help you get started.

If you've got no immediate work at hand, you can still start practicing your anti-procrastination skills right away. What you do is you look around: are there any chores that you can do - especially those that you've been putting off in the past. You can do the dishes, weed the garden, arrange your library, tidy up your room, send that email, etc.

All you have to do is break them into tiny bits - as discussed in chapter 35: one barrel at a time - and start executing the bits one after the other, then ensure you finish it up that day. If you do complete it, it will instill in you some elation and excitement about yourself, which pumps you up for more action. In contrast, studies have shown that the habit of procrastinating and low self-esteem often go hand in hand together.

Link to study:
https://www.ncbi.nlm.nih.gov/pmc/articles/PMC4359724/

The more you indulge in task delaying behavior, the lower your self-esteem would get. So, catch yourself while procrastinating and take action immediately. The more action you take, the more confident you will feel to take more action. It's an upward spiral of confidence and productivity.

> *"Start where you are. Use what you have. Do what you can."* –
> **Arthur Ashe**, American tennis player, winner of three grand slams.

Summary

• To catch yourself procrastinating is one of the most important steps in getting started.

• Be mindful of your actions as you go about your day.

• When you find yourself avoiding a task, acknowledge the fact. Pick up your gear and start working.

• Use the techniques mentioned in this book to help you get started.

Section – II
How To Take Consistent Action

Once you get comfortable with starting a new task or habit, the next obstacle you might face is a lack of consistency. You don't follow through on a daily basis.

Suppose you started exercising. That's a great first step to getting fit. But maybe you aren't able to exercise regularly. You skip many days in between. This irregularity would make it hard to get good results in your fitness.

It is the same with building a business, getting good grades, improving your relationships, and changing habits. Taking consistent action is the key to success in all those areas.

Any worthwhile goal will require you to put in consistent effort over a period of time. If you do not persist regularly, it would be hard to achieve what you desire.

In this section, we will discuss some of the best techniques and strategies to improve your consistency. By applying these methods, you'll be able to follow through and take action daily until the objective is attained.

23. Forward Momentum

The Problem

Have you ever wanted to build a new habit or a routine, but gave up because you didn't believe you'd be able to maintain it for long? For example, have you ever wanted to start a new diet and exercise routine but gave up the idea because you didn't believe you could keep it up?

We have all been there.

We often think it's easy to start something and hard to keep it going? Actually, it is the opposite. Getting started is the hardest part. Once you begin something and do it for a few days, it actually gets easier to keep it going.

How does this work? Let's take a look.

The Procrastination Solution

Momentum fuels persistence.

Momentum is the "flow" you have when you are taking action consistently. For instance, if you are already going to the gym five days a week, it will not be difficult to work out six days a week. Because you are already taking action, you have forward momentum. It works on the principle, *"it's much easier to keep a ball rolling, than to get it moving from a standstill."*

That's why starting something new is harder than keeping it going. It takes a lot more effort to initiate something. But once it picks up momentum, it's easier to maintain.

In a research paper published by Seppo E. Iso-Ahola and Charles O. Dotson, psychological momentum (PM) plays an important role in goal pursuit and achievement.

"A long research tradition suggests that psychological momentum (PM) plays a critical role in goal pursuit and achievement. Accordingly, sequential runs of success are an essential feature of high levels of performance, meaning that better performers perceive and experience momentum of success more frequently, ride it as long as they can, and as a result, become more successful in the end."

Link to study:
https://www.ncbi.nlm.nih.gov/pmc/articles/PMC5006010/

Momentum is incredibly helpful in being consistent. If you are just starting out and want to build forward momentum, break down the large goal into a series of smaller steps. Smaller steps demand less effort from you. The less effort is required, the more work you do. The more work you do, the more momentum you gain.

For instance, if you want to lose weight, start drinking green tea every morning instead of coffee and be persistent with that. After a few days, add 30 minutes of walk in your day. Soon after that, replace oily and fried food with green vegetables.

Take it easy in the beginning. Start small and do activities that require only a little effort. Once you feel comfortable, begin taking up challenges which demand more. For example - eat only healthy food, cut out all sugar and processed food, exercise regularly, strictly following your schedule, etc.

As you complete smaller challenges, you will start gaining momentum. It will become increasingly easier to take action regularly. Soon, you'll reach a point where it will be easier to keep going than to stop.

And this will have a spill-over effect on all areas of your life. Momentum is energy, and by practicing it, you are putting energy into your everyday life. You will feel more alive and vibrant. The joy of taking down challenges, coupled with satisfaction from moving in the direction of your desires, will create such a high, you will not want to stop.

At such a point, the power of momentum is really on your side. You will breeze past any obstacles & problems without giving a second thought. It's like shifting to the fast lane to success. Moving forward will become your default way of thinking and behaving.

Here is one thing you have to keep in mind. Just as momentum is gained through taking action, it can decrease or even die out if you stop for too long. You have to keep taking action regularly to build and sustain healthy levels of momentum. Do not think once you gain momentum; it will continue on its own forever. If you stop, momentum will start decreasing, and with time, it will fade away.

Keep both of these factors in mind:

a) taking frequent action creates and sustains momentum.

b) being stagnant will kill momentum.

Use this knowledge to your advantage and never lose your momentum. The higher your momentum, the stronger your persistence will be.

"Often, the only difference between winning and losing is momentum. It solves 80% of your problems." – **John C. Maxwell**, author, speaker, and leadership expert.

Summary

- Many people give up creating a new habit or routine because they don't believe they will be able to maintain it.

- In reality, starting something new is harder than keeping it going. It takes a lot more effort to initiate a new habit or routine. Once you get started, the power of momentum comes into play.

- Momentum is the "flow" you have when you are taking action consistently. It works on the principle, *"it's much easier to keep a ball rolling, than to get it moving from a standstill."*

- Don't be afraid of not being able to maintain consistency. Actually, once you start something and do it a few times, it becomes easier to follow through.

- Use strategies in the first section this book to help you get started. Once you get the ball rolling, you will be surprised how simple it is to be persistent.

24. "Don't Break The Chain" Technique

The Problem

We all have heard "consistency is key." We get it. What you do every day, matters more than what you do once in a while. One burger won't make you overweight. Watching one movie won't make you unproductive. It is the repetition that determines the outcome.

The Procrastination Solution

Don't break the chain is a popular technique to overcome procrastination and take action consistently. It's also called the 'Jerry Seinfeld method' as it was coined after the popular actor-comedian.

This technique is popular because of its simplicity. You only need a calendar and a red-ink pen. First, you decide on an activity that you want to do daily. As you perform the activity each day, put a large red mark (X) on the calendar.

As you continue to take action and mark each day on the calendar with a red (X) sign, a chain of red X will form in the calendar. Try your best to not break this chain. Keep the chain going as long as you can.

Why It Works?

Each red X on the calendar is a visual cue of successful completion of the chosen activity. It represents progress, growth, and consistency. Every X is a small victory. It activates the reward system in the brain. It feels extremely rewarding to see the chain get longer each day. You will put extra effort to ensure that the streak continues.

And before you know it, performing the activity will turn into a daily habit. It'll become second nature. Now, there's no need to mark it in the calendar. You'd do it without thinking.

This technique works best for building new habits and taking consistent action. If you are looking to turn any activity into a daily habit, *don't break the chain* is an excellent option.

Putting It Into Action

Example #1 - Suppose you want to make exercise a daily habit. Do the exercise today and put a red X mark on today's date in the calendar. When you do the exercise tomorrow, again put a red X in the calendar. Repeat it every day. Don't break the chain.

Example #2 – Maybe you want a habit of reading a book for 30 minutes every day. The process is same. Read a book for 30 minutes today and put a red X mark on today's date in the calendar. Repeat it daily. Keep going until it becomes a habit.

Definitely give this one a try!

> *"Knowledge, if it does not determine action, is dead to us."* – **Plotinus**, Roman Philosopher.

Summary

- Select an activity that you want to turn into a daily habit.

- When you do it each day, mark the date on the calendar with a red (X) sign.

- Every (X) represents the successful completion of the activity.

- It activates the reward system in the brain, resulting in increased motivation.

25. The Recovery-Management Principle

The Problem

One of the most common problems my clients face is a decline in their motivation level. Many people start strong but quickly lose their drive to accomplish their goals. It hinders their consistency. *"What should I do to increase my motivation?"* is one of the most frequent questions I encounter.

The Procrastination Solution

Whenever a person loses their motivation, they start contemplating whether they are really passionate about their goal or not? They take a good, hard look at their work and try to figure things out.

In my experience, the reason behind losing your motivation is not the work itself; it's *the time between the tasks*.

As we go through our day, there are lots of things which demand our attention like work, family responsibilities, hobbies, friends, etc. Going through our daily grind, we tend to forget about our goal.

The human mind has a tendency to put things in the background if it's not something which demands immediate attention. And because goals normally require some time to accomplish, it tends to get 'out of focus' for the majority of the day. This causes a loss in the intensity of motivation.

Let's suppose you reviewed your goals in the morning and felt really excited. You started the work with enthusiasm. But later during the day, you get caught up in some other work-related issue or maybe a friend needs your urgent help.

It's very common to forget about your goal when you get caught up in the daily grind. It causes a loss in motivation and worse, you start to get thoughts like - "oh, I cannot focus on my goals for long. Maybe I am just not cut out for this kind of thing" or "I keep forgetting about my goals, maybe they are not so important to me?"

It takes a toll on your feelings of desire. Slowly but surely, your motivation starts going down.

The solution is to be careful about how you spend the time between your work periods.

Whenever you have some free time, immerse yourself in pictures, audio & information of your objective on daily basis. Read books, listen to audio, view pictures, read information about your selected goal.

For example, if your goal is to buy a brand new Volkswagen Jetta, read its reviews, go to its website, read glowing ownership experiences, watch long ride videos on YouTube, read about its earlier models and technical advancements.

Try to deliberately and knowingly expose yourself to your desire so you can see it, hear it, and read about it. It will make sure your goals are in your mind all the time. Whenever you have some free time, instead of watching random videos, watch something related to your goal - any new information, review, people's opinions, how other people achieved it and so on.

It can be a video, book, songs, audio program, pictures or anything else related to your goal.

But to clear things up; it does not mean that you should watch videos all day and not take action. It is meant to be done in spare time; in place of other unneeded activities that we do when we get free.

For example, you want to grow your business and have scheduled marketing work from 11.00 am to 4.00 pm, do not waste your precious work time by reading an article about the luxurious lifestyle of big business owners.

When it's time to work, do your work with full concentration. When you get some free time to do other activities, you can choose to spend it reading/watching anything about your goals.

It's your answer against distractions and negative influences. That's another positive aspect of this idea. It protects you from indulging in some activity which may cause you to be distracted for the whole day. It guards your mind against other negative influences like gossiping, reading rumors, and wasting time on social media because you are spending your free time focusing on your goal.

As you can imagine, being careful of your free time can boost your concentration, productivity, and motivation to a much higher level. In my own experience, it drastically improved my focus. Regardless of the activity, I'd be doing, my goals were on my mind. My clients love it. Many told me that ever since they started doing this, they've noticed a substantial increase in their motivation. It's time you adopt this strategy for your benefit as well.

> *"The successful warrior is the average man, with a laser-like focus"* – **Bruce Lee**, actor and legendary martial artist.

Summary

- During breaks, immerse yourself in pictures, videos & information about your goals.

- It will refresh your focus and boost motivation levels.

26. Find Your Biological Rhythm

The Problem

In today's culture, we are bombarded continuously with messages like *"hustle 24/7," "no pain, no gain," "work 80-90 hours a week."* Society encourages constant action with as little rest as possible.

However, there is a very real issue with this ideology. Constant action without rest can lead to feeling exhausted. It could make you think, *"I cannot continue any longer"* or *"it's just all too much."* It is often the reason behind your inconsistency. What should we do in this situation?

The Procrastination Solution

The world celebrates action. Any type of rest and relaxation is looked down upon. But in reality, both are necessary. One cannot exist without the other. All top-performing athletes know the importance of recovery. They train as hard as possible and then allow their body to recover. It helps them reach their peak mental and physical capabilities.

"I think the biggest thing for all athletes is recovery – being able to bounce back from week to week, practice to practice, to come back in top form" – **Larry Fitzgerald**, American pro footballer.

If we want to work with maximum efficiency, we need a balance between action and recovery. Focusing solely on taking action and not giving ourselves enough time to recover can lead to all sorts of problems like tiredness, laziness, exhaustion, and burnout. There should be a balance. You don't always need to work. Sometimes it better to shut down, put your feet up, and rest.

What Science Says

When we talk about rest, many people believe it's about getting enough sleep. But there's more to it.

Chronobiology is a specific field of science that helps us understand a number of biological rhythms which govern our body functions. For example, circadian rhythms are 24-hour cycles that influence functions like sleep and waking up. Infradian rhythms are longer than 24 hours. An example would be: women's menstrual cycles, which occur over the course of the month.

There are many biological rhythms in our body, but for productivity, we will focus on one specific type - Basic Rest Activity Cycle (BRAC in short).

Physiologist Nathaniel Kleitman, who pioneered sleep research, suggested that BRAC is a biological rhythm that lasts for around 90 minutes (between 80 to 120 minutes). The brain is quite focused and creative during the 90-minute duration. Afterwards, the brainwaves slow down for the next 20 minutes, making you feel drowsy and tired.

Here's how it works:

90 minutes - you are alert and focused.
20 minutes – You feel drowsy and tired.
90 minutes - you are alert and focused.
20 minutes – You feel drowsy and tired.

And it repeats infinitely.

This rhythm is working all day and all night within the body and has a profound impact on our life. It would be wonderful if we can somehow put it to use to boost our productivity.

Putting It Into Action

We have already discussed that our brain performs best for 90 minutes and unwinds for the next 20. Here's what you can do. Try to schedule your work in 90-minute intervals. Work during the full 90 minutes when the brain is most alert, focused, and creative. You'll be able to solve problems better. You'll have a clearer vision and make better decisions.

For the next 20 minutes, let your brain relax and recharge itself. For instance, get up from your chair and go take a sip of water from the water cooler. Maybe strike up a fun conversation with a friend/colleague. Listen to some soothing music. Take a short walk outside. Do relaxing activities.

After 20 minutes are up, repeat the sequence.

By working in 90-20-minute cycles, you are allowing your brain to function according to its natural rhythm. That's how it was designed by nature. Fully alert, focused, and creative for the 90 minutes. Relaxed for the next 20 minutes.

For instance, write your report for 90 minutes and relax for 20 minutes. Do your homework for 90 minutes and rest for 20. Do coding for 90 minutes and take a break for 20 minutes.

Obliviously, it requires a flexible work schedule. Some people may not have the leeway to take a break every 90 minutes. But if your work schedule allows for flexibility, give this strategy a go. You will notice a sharp boost in productivity. You will feel more energetic and creative during the work sessions. You will make better choices, think long term, and come up with innovative solutions to problems.

This approach is widely gaining popularity, especially among solopreneurs and students. Their schedule tends to be flexible enough to accommodate this strategy. If you can set your own schedule, try it and see how much of a difference it makes!

"Sometimes the most urgent and vital thing you can possibly do is take a complete rest." – **Ashleigh Brilliant**, author and syndicated cartoonist.

Summary

- Constant action with little rest leads to exhaustion and burnout. Taking a rest is vital.

- Rest means more than having enough sleep.

- The biological rhythm, BRAC, causes our brains to be alert and focused for approx. 90 minutes and restful for the next 20.

- Try to schedule your work in 90-minute intervals. Take a break for 20 minutes to rest & recover.

- When adopting this approach, you are allowing your brain to function according to its natural rhythm.

- Provided your schedule is flexible, taking this approach can create a noticeable difference in your productivity.

27. The Power Of Inner Equilibrium

The Problem

A distressed mind might be the reason you are not taking action consistently.

Our brain behaves differently under the influence of negative emotions like stress. Suppose you are trekking through a forest and a vicious bear charges at you. It will immediately trigger the "fight or flight" response in your body. The brain will shut down any physical processes unnecessary in this situation and direct all energy, oxygen, and blood flow to your legs and other organs allowing you to run away to safety.

This is a biological mechanism built inside every human being. This is why you cannot think properly when you are under a lot of stress at work or home. The more intense the emotion, the more distorted your mind will become.

There is a lot of truth in the old saying, *"Never make a decision when you are angry."* Intense emotions like anger, fear, and anxiety significantly compromise your ability to process information and make rational decisions. It'd be wise to time-out and get relaxed before tackling any critical issue at work or home. Negative emotions block your ability to think rationally.

In order to make good decisions and be productive, we need more positive emotions in our day.

The Procrastination Solution

The general consensus is that happiness follows success. Once we become successful, then we will be happy. There is no other way.

If that were true, then everyone would just work non-stop until they achieve their goal and live happily ever after. We all know, and several pieces of research prove, that it doesn't work that way. If we look around, we can find several examples of people who had all the money, all the fame, all the admiration they wanted, yet still resorted to drugs and alcohol to feel happy.

A long-term study examined the effect of happiness on its participants' careers. The researchers measured the optimism levels of participants when they first entered college. 19 years later, the participants were again measured on three criteria – current income, job satisfaction, and unemployment history.

Its analysis shows that individuals with a higher happiness rating at college entry had a higher income and a higher job satisfaction rating later in their careers. They are less likely to have been unemployed than individuals with a lower happiness rating.

Link to study:
https://link.springer.com/article/10.1023/A:1019672513984

Additionally, Gallup-Healthways Well-Being Index shows that unhappy employees take 15 more sick leave days in a year. Essentially, happy people have better health, a better immune system, and are resistant to mental disorders like depression & anxiety.

Happier people are also found to be more productive than average. In a 2010 study, James K. Harter and colleagues concluded that low job-satisfaction and happiness at the workplace resulted in poorer bottom-line performance. When people are unhappy, they don't show up consistently, they are less productive, or their work quality suffers.

A lot of research suggests that employees' emotional life has a big impact on their creativity, productivity, commitment, and problem-solving ability. Employees are more likely to have new ideas and insights when they feel happier.

Conventional wisdom advocates that pressure improves performance, but actual data shows that workers perform better when they are *happily* engaged in what they do.

A Powerful Exercise to Increase Your Happiness and Positivity

The last section of this book provides several ways to manage your thoughts and emotions. However, I would like to mention one specific exercise that made a significant impact on the amount of happiness my clients and I experience on a daily basis.

When you wake up in the morning, write down five things you are grateful for.

For example, when you sit down in the morning to drink your morning coffee/tea at the office, take out a notebook, and write five things you are grateful for in your life. Do it daily for 21 days.

A few pointers for this exercise:

1. These five things could either be big or small. It doesn't matter. It could even be something as simple as "*I am grateful for this morning coffee. Thank you.*"

No matter how small or simple the thing you are grateful for, it still counts. As you continue to do this exercise, your creativity would kick in, and you'll come up with various things to feel grateful for.

2. It is important to write down these five things on a piece of paper (notebook, diary, notepad, etc.). Writing them digitally on electronic devices does not count. They should be written by hand on real paper with a pen.

This is an important step. Writing on paper with a pen influences our brain very differently than typing on a keyboard. Make sure you use a pen and paper while doing this exercise.

Tip: Keep a pen & notebook at the place where you drink morning coffee (or at any other place you selected for this exercise). It must very handy and convenient to just pick up the pen & paper and start writing.

3. If you are not in the mood to do this exercise, tell yourself that it takes less than five minutes. It will be over before you finish your coffee.

4. You have to do this daily for 21 days. It takes 3 weeks for our brain to develop new neurological pathways. In other words, it takes 3 weeks for the brain to rewire itself and create the habit of positivity and happiness. Do the exercise every day for three weeks.

Soon, you will start noticing that your overall mood is getting better. As you go about your day, you will start noticing more things to be grateful for. You will start waiting for the morning because the gratitude exercise fills you up with good, happy emotions that carry over to the entire day.

"Success is not the key to happiness. Happiness is the key to success." - **Albert Schweitzer**, *theologian, writer, philosopher, and physician.*

Summary

- Negative emotions like anger, fear, and anxiety block your ability to think rationally.

- Research shows that people perform better and are more productive when they are **happily** engaged in what they do.

- A proven exercise to boost happiness and satisfaction is to write down five things you are grateful for when you wake up in the morning.

- Do this exercise daily for 21 days because it takes around 3 weeks for our brain to develop new neurological pathways and form new behaviors.

28. Let Food Be Thy Medicine

The Problem

When we talk about taking action consistently, we rarely give thought to the food we eat. The busier we are, the less importance we place on food. In social media, it's trendy to post how someone skipped a meal because of their busy schedule. It is perceived as an admirable quality.

But as it turns out, that is often the wrong approach. The foods we eat (or don't eat) affect us more than we think. Food has an immediate impact on our energy levels & focus, which is why a poor choice of food at breakfast or lunch can spoil the entire workday. Lack of energy, resulting from poor nutrition, can easily lead to an unproductive day.

The Procrastination Solution

Pay close attention to what you eat. Your concentration problems, lack of energy, mental fog, and similar issues can often be traced back to your eating habits. Contrary to the work culture around us, food is not an inconvenience. It is the fuel for your mind and body. A lot of studies have found a direct association between cognitive functions and nutrition.

What Science Says

In the research article "Brain Foods: the effect of nutrients on brain function," Fernando Gomez explained that diets that are high in saturated fats are becoming recognized for reducing molecules that support cognitive processing and increasing the risk of neurological dysfunction.

Link to the research article:
www.ncbi.nlm.nih.gov/pmc/articles/PMC2805706

And it's not only saturated fats. Simple carbohydrates like white rice, sugar, refined flour have an immediate effect on our energy and brain function. The food we eat is converted into glucose by the body. But not all foods are processed at the same rate.

When you eat high amounts of carbohydrates, especially simple carbohydrates like white rice, sugar, refined flour, it gets digested and converted into glucose quickly, resulting in a sudden spike in glucose levels in the body. Although the human body needs glucose, it requires the glucose levels to remain at a consistent level.

When the body detects the high spike in glucose level, it produces insulin to reduce the glucose levels back to normal. This phenomenon is known as hypoglycemia or sugar crash. A sugar crash can disrupt productivity and energy levels for several hours, if not the entire day.

The solution is to start adding more fiber-rich foods that get processed slowly in the body, providing steady energy levels throughout the day. Try adding more fresh fruits and vegetables to your diet. An easy way to do that is to add a green salad to eat with every meal.

Reduce your sugar intake as much as you can. Stop eating fried, deep cooked, or barbecued foods. Eat the right kinds of carbohydrates. Shift from simple carbs to complex carbs, which break down slowly in the body.

Drink at least two to four liters of water daily depending on the weather conditions you live in and the amount of physical activity you do. The more extreme the weather, the more water you need to preserve your water level. Drinking two to four liters of water is considered safe by many experts.

You don't need much protein. The recommended amount is - 0.8 to 1 grams per kilogram of your body weight in a day. And while it's possible to get all 20 different kinds of proteins entirely from plant sources, it'll be a little challenging. You can add a small amount of dairy or clean meats like chicken to your main fruits and vegetable diet. This will ensure that you get the whole range of amino acids easily.

Nutrition is a vast subject that is beyond the scope of this book. The point of this section is to remind you that if you eat a balanced diet with a wide range of fruits and vegetables, it will do wonders for your energy levels and productivity.

> *"Health is like money. We never have a true idea of its value until we lose it."* – **Josh Billings**, American author, humorist, and lecturer.

Summary

● Food has an immediate impact on your body and brain functions.

● Eating healthy food can result in a substantial boost to your productivity.

29. The Best Investment For Energy & Focus

The Problem

Taking action consistently is not simple. It demands a lot from you. If you don't have enough mental and physical energy to undertake this action, then it'll feel like you are fighting an uphill battle. It would be difficult to follow through on a daily basis. This is a very common, yet overlooked, reason behind procrastination. Lack of energy or fatigue can certainly make you postpone work.

It's imperative that we address it directly. What are some of the things can we do to boost our energy levels?

The Procrastination Solution

An active lifestyle not only changes your body, but it also changes your mind, your attitude, and your mood. Only a healthy body can sustain a healthy mind. And if you want your mind to be at its most resourceful, productive state… then physical activity is a must.

Physical movement increases blood flow to all parts of the body, including the brain. It results in an increased supply of oxygen and nutrients that serve as fuel for the brain. A plethora of hormones are also released that play a part in sharpening cognitive functions in the brain.

What Science Says

In a recent study done by the Department of Exercise Science at the University of Georgia, it was found that even exercising for 20 minutes can lead to improved information processing.

But, that's not all. Exercise also stimulates the growth of brain nerve cells (called neurons) that support cognitive and behavioral brain functions.

What it means is, if you keep chilling out on the sofa all day, you are probably not giving your brain a chance to operate at its full potential.

Try observing people who sit continuously for 8 hours in the office. They come home groggy, fatigued, and unable to think clearly. I used to be one of them.

Many years ago, I was working in a corporate job. I could feel my mind going 'numb' after 2-3 hours of continuous sitting on the computer. I was not exercising at the time. It all added up and dropped my energy levels to the point that I didn't even want to talk to anyone. I could barely feel happy and enthusiastic about ANYTHING.

If you would have asked me to do any creative work, the only response you would have gotten was a 'blank stare.' There was just no way I could process complex tasks, be creative, and enthusiastic.

None of those things was possible.

After months of 'chronic fatigue,' I finally decided to do something about it. I started reading about exercising and how it not only changes the body, but affects the mind, attitude, and mood as well.

After discovering a ton of benefits, I decided to begin exercising.

I started doing 20 minutes of brisk walking in the morning AND getting up from my chair every 30 minutes during my office time. I basically added more *movement* to my workday.

The results were better than I expected. I started to feel better. My energy levels increased along with my mood and enthusiasm. I became more vibrant and involved. People in my office were surprised by the sudden change in my demeanor. Everybody started appreciating the new 'me.' I started getting lots of compliments from others (they probably wanted to motivate me to stay like this).

I never expected to have this much positive energy if I just moved around more. Frankly, it was quite surprising. I had read about how exercise PROVIDES energy instead of depleting it, but it's quite a revelation to actually EXPERIENCE it yourself.

I have maintained this lifestyle ever since. Now my morning routine consists of a thirty-minute walk and fifteen-minute meditation. It gives me mental and physical energy that lasts all day.

I highly recommend taking a minimum of thirty minutes daily for physical activity – walking, cycling, jogging, weightlifting, tai-chi, yoga – select anyone you like. Remember to check with your doctor before starting.

In addition to the above morning exercise, get up from your chair every thirty minutes to stretch your legs. Take a short walk around the office. Go to the water cooler, take a sip, and come back. The point is to get up and move a bit.

Try doing both of these for ten days. You would notice a great improvement in your energy levels. It rejuvenates your mind & body and greatly boosts your productivity.

And when you consider the long-term health benefits of an active lifestyle, it's really a no brainer.

"The first requisite of success is the ability to apply your physical and mental energies to one problem without growing weary" – **Thomas A. Edison**, Legendary inventor and businessman.

Summary

- Mental and physical fatigue may be the cause behind your procrastination habit.

- Try exercising for a minimum of thirty minutes every day.

- This is definitely one of the best ways to improve your energy level.

30. The Slumber Effect

The Problem

When we are trying to take consistent action, it can be tough to finish everything that we set out to do. We usually think, "*I would have finished everything if I had more time.*" But recent studies suggest otherwise. It is better to focus on managing your energy than worrying about the time.

You can find numerous strategies to get more work done in a day. For example, you can delegate non-critical tasks to someone else. But if you lack the energy to get through the workday, then being productive can be very challenging. It can easily cause procrastination.

Energy is the basis of productivity. The amount of physical energy you have then determines how much can you get done. When our physical energy slumps, so does productivity. That's why it is important to remember that when you master your energy, you then master your ability to take consistent action.

The Procrastination Solution

One of the most important things that will affect our energy is getting enough sleep. When you are well-slept, your mind is much sharper, alert and resilient. You have more focus which in turn, increases your overall performance during the day.

On the other hand, when you have not slept well, you will feel drowsy and irritable all day. Your willpower will decrease and your emotions will be all over the place. You would become prone to indulging in instant stimulation (like social media, TV, alcohol) which would eat up all your time. Sleep is one of those things which can either make or break your day. It is critical to get proper sleep at night.

National Sleep Foundation recommends that healthy adults need between 7 and 9 hours of sleep every night. Children under the age of 16 need even more sleep than adults for their growth and development. People over 65 also require 7 to 8 hours per night.

So, the question now becomes – just how much sleep is enough?

It depends on the individual. Every one of us is unique and has a different sleep pattern. Some people can function well on six hours of sleep while others may need eight hours to feel well-rested.

However, research on sleep shows that most people need between seven to eight hours of proper sleep for optimum health and functioning. I personally need around eight hours of sleep. When I am well-slept, I feel refreshed and energized all day.

Try getting up at different times to find your own unique sleep requirement. You would eventually end up somewhere between seven to eight hours. Whatever your need is, then aim to get that many hours of sleep every day.

Don't be afraid of losing your productivity time. Some people think sleeping eight hours is a waste of time. Not really. You will be a LOT more productive in the daytime. You will have increased energy & alertness throughout the day. That one hour of extra sleep will result in several hours of increased performance. It's a worthy trade-off.

One more thing - it's not only the quantity of sleep that is important. "Quality" is also critical. Here are a few pointers on improving the quality of your sleep:

- Do not eat a heavy meal late at night.

- Avoid computer and mobile screens, TV, and bright lights one hour before sleep.

- Do relaxing activities before bed. Read a book, write a journal, etc.

- Keep the temperature of the bedroom cool and comfortable.

- Invest in a good quality mattress and pillows.

- Fix a time to sleep.

- Try to sleep in a completely dark room. Even dim light can interfere with the quality of sleep.

Get your sleep right. Without it, overcoming procrastination will be challenging. While it's certainly *possible* to be productive while being under-slept, it would be an uphill battle. We want our sleep to be an advantage, not a liability. Make efforts to improve your sleep and the rewards would be incredible!

"Tired minds don't plan well. Sleep first, plan later" – **Walter Reisch**, Austrian director and screenwriter.

Summary

- Proper sleep is a game-changer when it comes to improving productivity.

- The quality of your sleep is equally important as the quantity.

- Sleeping for seven to eight hours in a dark room is recommended for most people.

31. A Secret Energy Reserve That Can Double Your Productivity

The Problem

Have you felt mental fatigue at any time during work, even when you *could* go on physically? Have you ever found yourself *too* burned out to do something? Have you found that sometimes you are unable to focus on an activity?

All of these are caused by the depletion of energy. Having enough energy is one of the keys to taking consistent action. But there's more to energy than we believe.

The Procrastination Solution

When we talk about energy, we normally talk about physical energy; *"I am feeling tired," "I should take a nap," "Let's sit down for a minute."* Things like that are meant to relax and recharge the energy of our body.

What if I told you that another kind of energy needs recharging throughout the day – especially if you are doing a mentally challenging task – and this energy is equally or more important than the physical energy.

I call it – the emotional energy. It is the energy for the mind.

I discovered emotional energy while writing my first two books. Writing is very taxing on the mind as it requires a lot of brain processing power. When I was writing, I found that I am frequently burned out – even when I had enough physical energy to sit and write more.

I didn't feel physically tired, but I wasn't able to write. My brain just gave up after an hour or so of writing. I thought that if I lay down for a few minutes to rest, I would be able to work again.

I lay down on my bed and turned on the TV. After fifteen minutes, I felt rested enough. But when I start writing again, I couldn't get my mind to put down letters on the paper. Nope. I still couldn't write. I took a rest for an hour, thinking that my body needed more downtime.

But that didn't help either.

My mind was still unable to come up with new ideas and concepts. If I forced myself to write, the quality went down tremendously, and it just didn't felt right.

I thought maybe I just naturally had a very low writing capacity and couldn't write more than a few pages.

I tried many different things to improve it.

One day, I accidentally discovered that I could write more if I listened to my favorite songs for 10-15 minutes. Somehow it increased the quality AND quantity of my writing. I wasn't feeling as mentally burned out as before. I could write more WITHOUT taking hours of rest in between writing sessions.

As curious as I am, I started looking into this more and more. I found that the energy of the mind is different from the energy of the body. As the processes that relax the body are not as efficient in recharging the mind.

Sleeping eight hours at night recharges both body and mind, but if we need to do mentally complex work for several hours a day, emotional energy and its rejuvenation is the key.

Emotional energy is the energy used by the mind. Notice how I didn't just call it mental energy. There is a reason for that.

The mind uses emotions to recharge itself.

Yes. A quick nap also helps, but not to the same extent.

Now, does that sound pretty important?

It is!

I wonder why nobody talks about it.

Let's go into more details.

When I listened to a few of my favorite songs, I felt something. It was like my creativity was coming back to me. My mind felt a little, dare I say it, more alert.

That was the only time I felt something. It was not much, but it was the only clue I had at the time. I decided to find out more about it. I made a separate list of my favorite songs on my cell phone and listened to them for 30 minutes straight.

Afterwards, I felt somewhat better. It was not much improvement, but definitely better than before. I decided to delve deeper. I separated my favorite songs by the kind of emotions they summon inside. Some were sad songs, some were classical, some were upbeat… I like many different types of music.

I lay down on my bed and listened to my sad song collection first. Within 30 minutes, I was completely wrapped up in emotions generated by songs. It felt better but not by much. I was still feeling tired.

It was the same with classical music. I felt better but not by that much.

The moment came after I put on happy, uplifting music. After just 15 minutes of positive, uplifting music, I got up completely refreshed!!

And it was not just a little difference. I got up COMPLETELY refreshed.

It felt like a MIRACLE. If you have a kind of life where you often find yourself mentally exhausted, you could imagine how crazy good I felt after I discovered this.

My work required a lot of mental energy and I found a way to recharge it in little as 15-20 minutes.

I was ecstatic!

From that day, whenever I felt mental exhaustion, I just lay down on my bed and rocked my favorite uplifting music. It worked like a charm for me every time.

How much of a difference did it make, you ask?

Well, I used to give up after writing around 1500 words in a day, now I was able to write 4000-5000 words in one day!

It was an unbelievable jump in quality and quantity.

What's more, I felt a lot better during my day job as well. I was able to focus more on the tasks I did and was getting a lot more done. Everybody started noticing the change in me. My friend asked me if I started taking any supplements.

People wanted to know what changed. How did I become so productive and full of energy all of a sudden?

I felt it too – the change – and it was not because of multivitamins.

Now we come to the most important part in all of this – How to rejuvenate your emotional energy when you feel exhausted?

Solution: Generate emotions of happiness

Your emotional energy recharges every time you feel happy. Songs are an amazing way to generate feelings of happiness without much effort. I found that when I listened to happy, uplifting music, I instantly felt rejuvenated. After 15-20 minutes of music, I can continue mentally demanding tasks that I would have left alone for the day.

It is just not about music. Everybody is different. You may feel the same amount of happiness and joy by playing with your pets, taking a walk in the park, or talking to a loved one.

That is why I think of it as "emotions of happiness" and not "listen to upbeat music."

It is not about songs. It is about any way you can generate feelings of happiness inside yourself. Any method you choose is fine as long as it makes you happy.

Songs work the best for me. One of my clients feels equally joyful talking to his girlfriend on the phone. Another feels amazing by doing physical exercise. One watches comedy videos on YouTube and laughs out loud the whole time.

And for some people, even a forced laugh for one minute works wonders.

Everybody is different. You have to find your own way to make yourself feel happy. When you feel happy and excited, it brings out the emotions that get buried when we feel mentally exhausted. We feel energized, rejuvenated. We feel alive and vibrant. We feel like we can do anything now.

Try this for yourself. This one idea has made a huge positive impact on my overall productivity levels. It usually costs nothing and has the potential to skyrocket your productivity.

> *"All life is an experiment. The more experiments you make, the better."* – **Ralph Waldo Emerson**, American writer, lecturer, and philosopher.

Summary

● Mental fatigue can be a huge obstacle to productivity.

● Positive emotions (like happiness) help in overcoming mental fatigue.

32. The Vertical Element

The Problem

The human body is quite complicated. A multitude of functions and processes are carried out within the body that require a lot of energy. If we are not supporting our body to work efficiently, it makes us tired and fatigued. As mentioned earlier, a lack of energy is a common culprit behind the inconsistency in taking action.

The Procrastination Solution

Continuing with the theme of increasing energy level, let's look at another factor that significantly affects your vitality - posture.

We have a group of muscles that work hard to keep our back in an upright position. These are called postural muscles. When we are slouching, these muscles have to work extra hard to support our back, gradually making them tired and sore. It can make us feel dull and fatigued.

Often, we don't give too much thought to posture. Everyone knows that having an upright posture is good but I believe we don't put enough emphasis on it as we should.

Research has shown how significantly posture affects our energy level and mood — both of which are critical for being productive.

A recent study done at San Francisco State University measured how posture affects the energy level of the participants. One hundred and ten university students with an average age of 23.7 rated their energy level before the study. This was their baseline energy level.

Now, students walked with slouched posture for two or three minutes and measured their energy level. Afterwards, the students were told to walk in opposite arm leg skipping motions (with a good posture) and rated their energy level again.

The collected data shows that after walking with a bad posture for only two-three minutes, students reported a noticeable drop in energy. But, interestingly, after the opposite skipping motion (good posture), all student reported a significant increase in their energy levels.

The study concluded that we can change our energy levels by altering our posture. The connection between mind and body is a two-way street. Our mind affects our body. And our body affects our mind.

So, it's time to take posture more seriously. It's not a "good-to-have" sort of thing. It is critical for living a healthy, happy, and productive life.

Having a good posture:

- Allows for proper breathing.
- Lowers stress on muscles, bones, joints
- Reduces wear and tear
- Improves blood circulation.
- Improves mood.
- Can boost testosterone which affects your drive and focus.

Tips to Improve Your Posture

1. Sit straight in a chair. Use back support cushions or invest in a chair with solid back support.

2. If you exercise with weights, work on your back muscles at least once a week.

3. In my experience, a great way to improve posture is to practice yoga. It is unbelievably good for improving the body's flexibility and strengthening the core. Look for a yoga class near you.

4. Visiting a licensed chiropractor is another excellent option as they can properly assess your posture plus help you resolve any issues.

Overall, the point I wanted to make is that working on your posture is not optional. It is one of the foundational factors that allow us to feel happier, live healthier, and be more productive. It significantly affects your drive, focus, energy, mood, motivation, and health. Need we say more?

Make a conscious effort to improve it and reap the rewards forever.

"A good stance and posture reflect a proper state of mind" – **Morihei Ueshiba**, legendary Japanese martial artist and the founder of the martial art of Aikido.

Summary

- Research shows that our posture significantly affects our energy level and mood – both of which are crucial for overcoming procrastination.

- Use any of the four strategies provided above to improve your posture.

- A good posture allows us to feel happier, live healthier, and be more productive.

33. The Principle Of Time-Acceleration

The Problem

It is easy to take a day off when we have excess time. We feel relaxed when things are not too urgent. But while being relaxed doesn't sound too bad, it can lead to unnecessary delays and inconsistent action.

For instance, a sales executive is procrastinating on preparing a sales report because they have to submit it next week, or a student can't get themselves to study because the tests are three months away.

We tend to delay things when we think there is more than enough time. Usually, we start working at the very last minute. But usually, by that point, there's not enough time left. Either we do not finish the work or cut corners in the quality.

It is a universal problem. Everyone struggles with it at times.

The Procrastination Solution

One of the most recognizable traits of consistent action takers is a *sense of urgency*. They do their best to get things done as quickly as possible. Once they decide what needs to be done, they work relentlessly until it gets finished.

They ignore all distractions because they realize time is a limited resource. They have a burning desire to do as much as possible in a day. For them, comfort is the enemy.

It applies to people, organizations, and even countries. For instance, Japan's economy was devastated after World War II. Extreme measures, together with a sense of urgency, were required to bounce back from absolute chaos. That's exactly what happened. In the 1960s, Japan achieved one of its fastest recorded growth rates in GDP, shocking the whole world.

Bill Gates, the co-founder of Microsoft, mentions in his book *The Road Ahead* that "we (Microsoft) worked every day as if we are on the verge of losing the business. It gave us a sense of urgency and a drive to become the best in the market."

Fast actions bring quicker results. Having a sense of urgency will separate you from everyone else. Once you decide what needs to be done, do it now.

A sense of urgency is excellent at overcoming excuses like, "*I don't know when to start*," or "*I don't know how to do it*," or "*I don't feel like doing it*." When you really *have* to do something, you always find a way to get it done. It's a great tool for eliminating the habit of excuse-making.

Creating a Sense of Urgency

Now that we established the importance of having a sense of urgency, let's look at some of the best ways to create it:

1. One of the keys to creating a sense of urgency is to view time as a precious resource. When you view time as scarce, it completely shifts your mindset. Your focus gets fixed on things you can do right now to get the results you want.

2. Think about the benefits of finishing the work. How it will feel afterwards? Would you feel mentally relaxed? Would you feel good about yourself for completing the task? Would you be able to enjoy other activities a lot more knowing your work is finished? Think about all the benefits that you can get.

3. Think about what you would lose if you don't do the work. How will it affect you mentally, physically, financially, spiritually? How will it affect your relationships and your loved

ones? Imagine going through another day thinking, "I could have done so much work yesterday, but didn't." Do you wish to spend another day feeling guilty?

4. Promise someone that you will finish your work by a specific *time-period*. For instance, tell your friend that you'll join a gym by next Sunday. Promise your mom that you will clean up your room today. Promise your spouse that you'll begin searching for a new job from tomorrow. When you make a promise to someone, you'll be afraid of disappointing them by failing to live up to your word.

5. Challenge yourself to finish the work in half the allotted time. For instance, if you'd normally take ten days to finish a task, challenge yourself to do it in five. Challenges bring out the best in people. You'd surprised at how much you can get done when there's not enough time left. Either you'll ignore all distractions and get hyper-focused, or end up finding creative ways to get more done in less time.

The above-mentioned techniques help in creating a sense of urgency. The only pre-requisite is to give them a proper shot. If you apply them diligently, they will continue to serve you for a long time. Remember, either you have a sense of urgency today, or feelings of guilt tomorrow. What will you choose?

"The trouble is, you think you have time..." – **Gautam Buddha**, spiritual teacher, religious leader, and philosopher.

Summary

- It is easier to procrastinate when we think there is enough time.

- Use the five methods to create a sense of urgency and take consistent action.

34. Core Of Time Management

The Problem

Many times, the reason behind our inconsistent behavior is a lack of organization; we don't have any roadmap in mind as to how to get things done.

Whenever you lack a routine, your mind tends to wander all over the place and, as a result, becomes susceptible to distractions. Getting things done without a routine is like trying to hit a moving target in complete darkness. It's hard to get anything done.

One way to get out of this predicament is to maintain some structure and routine throughout your day.

The Procrastination Solution

We are definitely creatures of habit.

We get up at nearly the same time. Brush our teeth & take a shower. Get ready and go to the office by the same route that we do every day. Meet & greet the same people.

Habits are our thoughts and behaviors that we indulge in repeatedly, without giving much consideration about them. These are almost automatic. Research on human behavior shows that more than 70% of what we do in our day is unconscious. Means we do not think much about it. Typical present-day activity for an average person resembles yesterday to a staggering degree.

There are only little variations in our day. Thus, we tend to maintain our routine without giving it much thought.

We all have a routine. It might be beneficial or detrimental to our productivity. But the surprising fact is that we often don't consciously create our routine. Most of the time, we start doing something just out of curiosity, and soon it becomes a routine. Now it feels so comfortable that we do not question whether we should do it or not. We go ahead and just do it.

How Are Routines Formed?

In the human brain, there are electrical signals called **neurons** that pass through a **network of pathways**. When we carry out an action or think a thought, neurons pass through a pathway connected to that specific thought or behavior.

As we continue to repeat that specific thought or action, more and more neurons pass through that mental pathway in the brain, making it bigger & stronger. The more you repeat a behavior, the more neurons pass through the mental pathway causing it to grow bigger and allowing more neurons to pass through.

After some time, the mental pathway connected to that thought or behavior becomes so strong, it makes the flow of neurons much faster and easier, making the thought or behavior effortless and thus, forming a habit.

The more we repeat a thought or behavior, the more it gets ingrained in the brain... till a point where it becomes a habit or routine.

Habits do change the brain biologically.

How to Create a Routine for Maximum Consistency?

Let's apply what we have covered so far to create a highly productive routine.

Step 1. You'll have to figure out what it is that you want to achieve. That is the first step. Once you determine your goal, only then will you be able to design a routine around it.

What are your goals? Do you want to grow your business? Lose weight? Improve your relationships? What do you want?

You might have several goals. In that case, choose a maximum of three to work on. Any more than that, you'll be spreading yourself too thin and won't make much progress in any of them. The lesser the number of objectives, the more you'll be able to focus on them.

Two or three are quite manageable.

Step 2. Make a list of tasks that are obligatory for you to work on.

It consists of things like dropping your kids at school, your day job, family responsibilities, paying bills, house chores, and things like that. These are your "must-do" activities.

Write them down.

Figure out the time it would take to complete such tasks and whether they can be delayed or delegated? For instance, things like chores allow flexibility of time — you can do them at any time you want during the day. But things like your day job or dropping your kids at school can't be rescheduled for later.

Find out what can be rescheduled and what's fixed.

Step 3. Now that you have everything laid out in front of you, schedule them in different time slots during the day that are convenient for you.

Next, you should fine-tune it. Look at what can be delayed or removed altogether. Make adjustments to it based on your requirements.

Once it is done, your primary objective is to stick to this schedule as closely as possible, and fine-tune it as needed.

When you are unable to complete all tasks in your schedule, it's often because you have set too many tasks on your schedule. Be realistic about how much you can accomplish in a single day. Let's not get carried away and over-burden ourselves.

The goal of a well-structured routine is not to overwhelm ourselves. The intent behind creating and following a routine is to add some structure to our workday. It is to have a general frame of reference of what we should be doing at any given time during the day.

In the end, no routine is perfect. Everyone is unique and has their own set of goals and obligations. Only you can come up with a routine that works best for you. Use the guideline provided above to create a routine based on your unique requirements and follow it as closely as you can. Soon, you'll become so accustomed to the routine that you won't even think about it. You will automatically start to follow the structure without paying too much thought to it.

> "You'll never change your life until you change something you do daily. The secret to your success is found in your daily routine." – **John C. Maxwell**, author, speaker, and leadership expert.

Summary

- A lot of times, you procrastinate because you lack a productive routine.

- In the absence of a routine, your mind tends to wander all over the place and, as a result, becomes susceptible to distractions.

- The more we repeat a thought or behavior, the more effortless it becomes... until it reaches a point where it becomes a subconscious effect.

- Use the exercise above to create a routine tailored to your specific needs.

- Once you have created a routine, follow it as closely as you can. Soon, you'd start following the structure without thinking about it.

35. One Barrel At A Time

The Problem

Another prominent reason behind our lack of consistency is that the task seems too big and overwhelming. For instance, a person decides to lose 25 pounds of weight. Now, weight reduction is a slow process. An average person typically loses 1-2 pounds per week if they follow the diet and exercise properly. As only 1-2 pounds of weight reduction is visible after a week of hard work and discipline, losing 25 pounds can seem too farfetched. It may be hard to imagine achieving that goal; often resulting in demoralization and a lack of consistency.

The same applies to writing a book or thesis, building a business, becoming an A-grade student, or improving your relationships. All are huge goals with slow visible progress. Even when you tried your best, it could still feel like you haven't made any significant improvements at the end of the day.

But we must remind ourselves that the achievement of any worthwhile goal requires consistent action over a period of time. Big goals need a bigger commitment. They demand more energy, time, discipline, and hard work.

That's what makes them seem overwhelming. They look too big! When you see Mount Everest from the first base, it seems impossible to reach its peak. It looks extremely far away.

That is the problem with every big goal. When you are at the starting line and look at the end goal, it seems unreachable. We start doubting whether we could ever attain it. We start thinking like, "I don't know if I can do it," or "what's the use of trying." This doubt often stops us from working towards that goal.

The Procrastination Solution

Here's a great solution to this problem - if you are starting out, break down the large goal into smaller ones. Small goals are more manageable. They demand less from you. The less effort is required, then the easier it would be to take action.

I recommend breaking down your main goal into daily goals. Focus on completing one day at a time. For instance, suppose my main goal is to write a book. I broke it down to a daily goal of writing 3000 words a day. If I can consistently achieve my daily goal of writing 3000 words, I would easily reach my end goal of finishing the book.

It makes the process look less intimidating. Writing 3000 words a day seems achievable. Writing an entire book doesn't. That is why it is better to have smaller daily goals instead of one gigantic end goal.

Taking it a step further, break down your workday into a series of one-hour sessions. Let me explain. If my daily goal is to write 5000 words, I divide my work hours into one-hour-long writing sessions. I focus on doing my best work possible for one whole hour. Then I take a break to refresh myself. The breaks usually last for 5 to 15 mins. Then I start another hour-long writing session. I typically go through 6 to 8 sessions every day.

Let's discuss its benefits. When your end goal is massive, you usually have trouble tracking your progress. It feels as if you are not making any progress. This problem is solved by the "small sessions" method. You can measure your progress in real-time by looking at the number of sessions you completed today.

Each session is a small victory. Completing each one represents a step forward to achieving your daily goals, which will move you closer to your end goal. For instance, if I complete 6-8 writing sessions today, I would easily reach my daily goal of 5000 words. If I keep hitting my daily goal, then my book (end goal) will be complete in no time.

Note: Later in the book, we will cover technical ways to track your progress. This specific approach is more feeling-based. It is about getting the feel of making progress. By completing smaller work sessions and daily goals, you'd feel like you have accomplished something today. That would increase your motivation to push hard towards your end goal.

We have turned the situation in which we are intimidated by a massive goal into one where we're excited and driven to take action. You can use this method to handle any intimidating task at the office or home.

Note: Make sure that nothing interrupts you during the one-hour work sessions. Put your phone on silent. Turn off all notifications. The point is to be hyper-focused for the whole session.

Give it a go and watch your productivity skyrocket!

> *"Journey of a thousand miles begins with one step"* – **Lao Tzu**, ancient Chinese philosopher and writer.

Summary

- Large, intimidating goals are often demoralizing.

- Break the goal down into daily and hourly goals.

- Completing each one - will make you feel more accomplished and motivated.

36. The Dilemma Of Disguised Advancement

The Problem

Sometimes, even after working diligently, we don't see any progress. Fear of failure starts creeping into our minds. We get disheartened and stop taking consistent action.

Lack of visible progress is a prevalent reason behind procrastination. It gives birth to fear of failure that kills our motivation to take action. What should we do in this situation?

The Procrastination Solution

Have faith.

Faith is one of the core pillars of strength against fear. Have strong faith in yourself, your vision and your ability to succeed. A strong, unshakable faith can move mountains, and a weak one can stop you from taking the next step.

Please realize that we are all very similar to each other. The richest and the most successful people have the same physical characteristics as you have. Nobody is cut from a different cloth.

We all have the same brain, body, and time. The basic foundation is the same for everyone. It's the way you use what you have been given, that makes all the difference.

> *"If you never try, you'll never know what you are capable of."* - **John Barrow**, English physicist.

Successful people use their resources on things like learning, training, taking action, finding solutions, making progress, etc.

Using their resources in a positive direction is what separates the best from the rest.

So believe in yourself and your vision. If you are reading this, you have access to enough resources to potentially become one of the most successful people in the world. You are more than enough at this very moment. Do not ever doubt yourself.

Think BIG!

Take action!

And have UNSHAKABLE faith!

It's all about how strong your faith is. It is the conviction with which you believe in yourself. Your faith, at any point, should never be anything less than unbreakable.

There are two reasons for it:

1. Nobody is cut from a different cloth. You have similar resources to the ultra-successful people.

2. A breakable faith is of no use at all.

The bigger your goal, the stronger your faith needs to be. Bigger goals require more time and effort. They also contain harder challenges. It's critical to operate with unshakable faith in such cases because it will be tested many times over.

> *"None of us knows what might happen even the next minute, yet still we go forward. Because we trust. Because we have faith."* **-Paulo Coelho**, author of *The Alchemist*.

You can come back to your faith during the tough times to take shelter from chaos & uncertainty. It's like an oasis in the vast desert. It is your place of certainty and calm. Strong faith has the power to keep you going even when it seems like all doors are closed.

Faith keeps you going.

Faith and fear cannot co-exist together. They cancel each other out. In your mind, there is a place for only one - faith or fear. And you get to decide which one exists. You are the creator. You have complete power over their existence. Use this gift in your favor.

> "*Faith and fear both have you believing in something which you cannot see... You decide.*" **-Bob Proctor,** world-renowned speaker and author.

Always have complete faith in yourself, your abilities, and your success. There is no reason you shouldn't have this faith. A lack of faith will weaken your resolve and ensure that you quit at the very first signs of difficulty and setback. On the other hand, an unshakable faith will guide you towards the life of your dreams.

Let your faith be bigger than your fear.

How to Strengthen Your Faith?

1. Start with your "why"

Identify the reasons behind what you feel and what you really want. If your "why" is important enough, you will keep a much stronger level of faith. You have to believe in the reason for which you want to succeed.

When your reason is important enough, you'll simply refuse to lose. The intensity of your desire is a big influence on how strong your faith is. So really connect yourself with your "why." Become attached to it emotionally. Feel its importance.

It will bring so much intensity to your desire that you won't even consider any possibility of it not happening.

2. Positive affirmations

Affirmations have been proven very beneficial for maintaining high levels of faith. Your mind is like a sponge. It starts to believe any thought which gets repeated on a frequent basis. Use it to your advantage. If done correctly, affirmations are super effective. For details on how to do affirmations, refer to the section on building beliefs.

3. Past success

If you have achieved success in the past, you tend to have greater faith in yourself. If you have been successful, take time to remember how you felt, how you thought, and what you did.

Remembering your success in a positive light will create faith in your mind - "*I have dealt with many obstacles before and have been successful. I'll make it this time as well.*"

4. Everyone is equal

Remember that successful people are just like you. They have the same time, energy, and challenges. It will strengthen your resolve. Many ultra-successful people have started their journey from a very low position - being broke, unhealthy, no education, no support, etc. If you are reasonably educated, healthy, and have enough resources to read this book, you have a great starting point.

5. Small progress

Your faith gets stronger as you take action and start making progress. People say they don't have enough faith to take action. They don't realize that as you take action and start seeing some progress, your faith starts to become stronger.

With your increased faith, you take even more action, which gets you even better results, which further strengthens your faith. It's like a continuous, upward cycle of strengthening faith.

6. Faith in God/Universe

Another strong source of faith is the feeling that some greater force is watching over you, and if you do your best, it will be repaid. Religious people think of such a greater force as God. If you are an atheist, you can think of it as the greater good or the universe.

Faith in a greater entity will make you relaxed and calm. When you believe there is a sense of justice in the world, and your efforts are being taken into account, you won't be too worried about the result. You will do your best and have faith.

> *"Your duty is to make your best effort, without worrying about the result... result will come."* - **Lord Krishna.**

Summary

- Lack of visible progress is a common reason behind inconsistent action.

- Faith and fear cannot co-exist together.

- Have unshakable faith that if you keep taking action, results will come.

- Do your absolute best without worrying about the results.

37. Discomfort Is Temporary

The Problem

When you are following through and taking consistent action, you might experience long periods of discomfort or even pain. It often leads to procrastination. What can we do in this situation?

The Procrastination Solution

You must persevere. Please remember that the discomfort is temporary. It may feel bad right now, but the eventual result will be well worth it!

And it's not solely about the result. Time and time again, after people achieve their goal, they value the hardship, the effort they have made, more than the actual outcome itself.

> *"True happiness is never the goal which you achieve, but the journey and the person you become who is able to achieve that goal."* **- Old proverb.**

Think of it as a purification of self. It's a rite of passage you have to go through to achieve your desire. The pain and discomfort might be here right now, and you hate it as much as possible, but later it will be the part that makes you the proudest.

I still remember a time when productivity literature was just a hobby of mine. At a certain point, I wanted a new corporate job with better pay. However, there was a catch. I was not looking for a small salary hike; I wanted to double my current pay. It was a lofty goal, and believe me; it led to some pretty rough times in the interviews.

As soon as the interviewers found that I wanted twice the salary, they said NO immediately, thinking I was either too entitled or arrogant. Some wanted to know the reason behind it, but after hearing my answer, they would generally say no.

Some laughed at me, and some told me to leave immediately. I was getting rejected left and right, but I kept it up. I knew I would find someone who will accept it. I kept doing interviews, kept trying different approaches. Finally, one interviewer said, 'OK.' There was an emergency vacancy they wanted to fill as soon as possible, and I fitted the bill pretty well, in spite of higher pay.

Luck? I do not think of it as luck. If I didn't have the courage to keep going to interviews even after getting rejected by everybody, I would never have landed an opportunity like that.

Action creates luck. The more action you take, the luckier you become. That's what happened to me.

And after all these years, if you ask me what I really cherish about that memory, my answer would be - my willingness to push forward even in the face of discomfort and rejection.

That feat is much more valuable to me than getting a bigger paycheck. Experiences like that shape the character of a person and, subsequently, his/her destiny.

True happiness is never the goals you achieve. It's always the person you BECOME during the process.

Work hard and do your best. What seems like pain or discomfort right now will become your most cherished memory later.

> "The truth is that our finest moments are most likely to occur when we are feeling deeply uncomfortable, unhappy, or unfulfilled. For it is only in such moments, propelled by our discomfort, that we are likely to step out of our ruts and start

searching for different ways or truer answers." – **M. Scott Peck**, American author, and psychiatrist.

Summary

- When taking action, you may feel periods of discomfort or pain.

- Think of it as a rite of passage you have to go through to achieve your desire.

- What seems like pain or discomfort now - will become your most revered memory later on.

Section III
What To Do When Your Work Is Uninteresting

After covering how to get started and how to improve consistency in the last two sections respectively, we are now going to tackle the next obstacle to productivity: Boredom.

At times, you'll find your work excessively boring. You won't have any passion for it and try to avoid it as best as you can.

Boredom is a very strong demotivator. It can have a serious repercussion on productivity. Because our brains are wired to seek pleasure, we are naturally repelled by tedious work. That's one of the reasons why we feel a strong urge to avoid such tasks.

According to Gallup's world poll, around 85% of the world's full-time workers are not engaged at work. Only 15% of the world's workforce like what they do. What a shocker!

This issue is so prevalent yet still not talked about in the media as it should. A popular message that's circulating in the mainstream media is *"find a job that you are passionate about."*

It's true. There is nothing better than finding work that you love. But what if you are stuck with a monotonous job? You may not have a choice to avoid dull activities. They still need to be completed no matter how you might feel. And it's not just in the office; many activities at home are super boring but unavoidable.

We must learn to handle tedious work. We need to equip ourselves with strategies that help us overcome task-related boredom. That's our focus in this section.

The strategies in this part will support you in overcoming procrastinating on tedious activities. No matter how boring you may find a task, using the methods outlined in this section will help you finish it.

38. Diamonds In The Rough

The Problem

Boredom is real, and truth be told, a lot of the stuff that you must do is going to be boring. For instance, imagine you have to study a 300-page research paper. This is not a novel we are talking about, but a monotonous stretch of technical work, articulately written by someone who isn't worried about arousing your interest or mood, but just to pass across the information. You may find it dull and boring, but you have to do it. There's no getting around it.

Similarly, if you find your job uninteresting, you still have to do it every day. In that case, the best option would be to switch jobs. But what if changing your job or the field is not an option for any reason? What can we do?

The Procrastination Solution

Earlier, we talked about how our brains are conditioned to always seek fun and pleasure, hence our constant lust for instant and immediate gratification. So, we have to admit; our brains perform better at remembering and memorizing those pleasurable things more than anything else. Can you still remember the entire story of Game of Thrones? It can already be assumed that your face is lit up right now. Can you remember some of the characters? The quotes? And this was a series that lasted 8 or 9 good years! So, the point is it's not the length of the material or activity that scares us or makes us bored; it's the dichotomy between pleasure and otherwise in our brains. In fact, some of us actually go back to watch and re-watch past GOT seasons! The same explanation goes for the reason why you will remember a good novel pretty easily, even years after reading it, no matter the number of pages.

The issue is that if work or activity is boring to you, it will be pretty difficult for you to derive meaning from it, to do the task or activity well. Then, what's the point in spending hours at drudgery and not derive anything concrete therefrom. You will feel that in the end, you just wasted your time. That explains why students spend hours in the library slaving through their books only to not perform well in tests.

You must find something you like about your work. Usually, the work we do has multiple layers. It consists of several parts. Some parts you like and some parts you hate. You'll have to take a deeper look between the layers and find parts that you like and focus on that aspect. Spend more time doing it.

You can even take a step further and ask your manager to assign more of those tasks to you and delegate the things you hate to someone, who is good at it. Suppose you dislike writing sales reports but enjoy creating beautiful PowerPoint slides for meetings. You can explain this to your manager and get sales reports delegated to someone, who is good at it, and you can take over their design work in return. It's a win-win for everyone.

When you do find things that you like, focus on them. Get good at them and, as soon as you see an opportunity, switch over to a job that specializes in the tasks you like.

How to Find Things That You Like About Your Work?

1. Try everything: As we discussed earlier, the work we do has multiple layers. You'll have to take a deeper look to find parts that you like. The way to do it is to try out new things. Unless and until you try everything at least a few times, you won't be able to properly assess whether you like it or not.

2. Look at your hobbies: Are there some parts of your work that resemble your hobbies? For example, suppose your hobby is meeting new people. How about the HR field or sales? Both involve meeting different people on a daily basis. If your hobby is reading or writing, then what about working on internal newsletters or blogs for your organization?

3. Think about your dreams: What do you daydream about being or doing? Some of my clients imagined themselves standing on stage in front of a crowd. Their interest could lie in sales, marketing, or PR as they would frequently get the chance to address a group of people. Ask yourself, what do you see yourself doing when you think about success? It contains strong hints about what you like.

4. Explore your childhood interests: What fascinated you during childhood? For example, one of my clients loved helping his siblings and other kids. To him, the feeling of helping others is exhilarating. He was working in finance and hated it. By examining his childhood interest, he switched over to financial consulting. Now he directly interacts with other people and supports them in improving their finances. He loves his new role! He says he can't wait to get to work.

You deserve work that you love. Because life is too short to live doing something you hate. I would suggest that your first priority should be to find work that you love. Money should only be considered afterwards. If you keep doing something you hate just because of good pay, yeah, your bank account would be happy, but not you.

Overall, the best option is to switch over to a field that you love. And if that's not possible, the next best thing is finding something you like about your current work and focus more on it.

> *"if you love only about 50% of the work you do, you are very fortunate. Nobody likes everything that they do. Most people*

hate their jobs. If you like even half of what you do, you are lucky." - **Jeff Bezos**, founder of Amazon.

Summary

● You may find your work dull and boring. That may lead to procrastination.

● The work we do has multiple layers. You'll have to take a deeper look to find parts that you like.

● Use the above-mentioned strategies to find work that you like.

● When you do find things that you like, focus on them. Get good at them and, as soon as you see an opportunity, switch over to a job that specializes in the tasks you like.

39. An Antidote To Boredom

The Problem

Any work can become boring if we find ourselves doing the same things over and over. We all crave new experiences and novelty to keep things fresh and exciting. Even when you have a job that you love, it's easy to get bored. Additionally, if your job isn't something you are passionate about, it's even easier for boredom to creep in.

Even everyday activities that we normally find fun and enjoyable can become lackluster if we do them repeatedly. As a result, we start trying to look for ways to avoid doing the work.

So, what should we do here? What if we find our work too dull? Is there a way to make a monotonous task more fun & interesting?

The Procrastination Solution

Here is the good news; it is possible to make even the most mundane activities engaging. But before we get into that, it should be noted that not all tasks are similar. There are different types of work. Some activities may require a lot of concentration and critical thinking and some of the other activities don't. Let's differentiate between them.

First, there are some activities which don't require a lot of thinking and concentration. Such activities include house chores, running errands, exercising, cooking, driving, etc. You can easily do them without paying too much conscious thought. For example; when you are cleaning your room, do you have to pay 100% attention to everything you do? You might pay *some* attention, but your mind is mostly busy thinking about other things. The same goes for tasks like cooking and running errands. You do not have to use *all* of your attention and concentration on these activities.

Now, let's look at the second type of work. These are the opposite of the ones above. These tasks require our full concentration and thought process. Some examples include: writing a report or book, studying, coding, reading, drawing, comparing, planning, assessing, etc. Tasks like these require our undivided focus and attention. It would be detrimental to let your mind wander and think about something unrelated while doing these activities. For instance, suppose you are writing an essay. Is it okay to think about what will happen in the next episode of your favorite TV series? You'll be too distracted to write anything. Let's look at another example. Suppose you are studying and your mind is preoccupied with the events of yesterday's baseball game. You probably won't get much out of your study session. It would be better to take a break and start again later. The same applies to coding, planning, and making art. These are your *full concentration activities*.

Now that we have defined the two types of work. Let's go through each one and discuss how to make them more intriguing.

Category #1: Casual Tasks - It doesn't require full concentration or critical thinking, i.e., house chores, running errands, exercising, cooking, driving, etc. Here's how to make such tasks more engaging.

1. You can use music to add more enjoyment to your work. Few things in the world put you in a good mood like music. No matter how boring the activity, playing your favorite music will make you feel great. You'll be having so much fun that you wouldn't even realize when the work is finished. For instance, you are cleaning the house, which is considered to be an incredibly dull activity. However, if you plug in your headphones and play your favorite songs, it completely changes the dynamics. You go from being bored to bobbing your head, tapping your foot, singing & dancing along with the songs. You'd have so much fun while getting stuff done! I suggest making a playlist of your favorite songs. It might take a bit of effort, but it's so worth it.

So, listen to your favorite music while doing any casual tasks that don't require your full concentration. It can transform any tedious activity into a fun-filled experience.

2.You can listen to audiobooks. If you love learning new things or reading an interesting story, listening to audiobooks is an excellent alternative to music. Depending on your preference, you can opt to listen to non-fiction books like self-improvement, business, biographies, or fiction books. The choices are numerous. There are so many good options for books, and almost all are available in the audiobook format. Audiobooks are getting more popular by the day, and one of the biggest reasons for their growth is that you can listen to them while doing work. You can listen to them while mowing the lawn, cooking food, or while running errands. It's a great way to add spice to any boring activities.

3.Put your favorite shows/streams/videos on TV or smartphone. This is similar to the two tips provided above. Watching your favorite TV shows, or streams, or videos is a great way to have fun while tackling mundane activities. For instance, you can play them on your TV or phone while doing cardio. As it doesn't demand too much concentration, you can end up consuming a lot of your favorite content while exercising. You wouldn't believe how fast the time went by and everything is finished so soon. It's a great way to abolish boredom and make work more engaging. (Note: *You can listen to music or radio while driving but watching a video is an absolute no-no.*)

4. Have a fun conversation on the phone. Having a lively conversation is another way to make tedious work more interesting. I recommend hands-free headphones with a microphone for convenience as it will make your hands free (I know! I know!) to work on the task. When you're having a lively conversation on the phone, the time seems to fly by. You'll be done before you know it. And it'll be so much fun. Try it. You would be pleasantly surprised.

5. Have a fun conversation with another person. This is an alternative to the above method. Instead of calling someone on the phone, have a fun conversation with a person next to you. Face-to-face conversations are something else entirely. If you can find someone with whom you connect, the fun you both can have is incredible. You can share stories and crack jokes. Think about how much fun you have while spending time with someone you totally connect with (i.e., your best friend). It's just like that. And you'd do it while getting things done. What more can we ask for?

6. Work together with a friend or group. Having a friend or two is always more fun than working by yourself. When you have other people around, you can chat with them, make jokes, and have fun. Another benefit is that when you see others doing their work, it inspires you to get your work done. Let's look at an example. You might find it boring to exercise alone. But when you have a group of friends around you while exercising, it will motivate you to get your full cardio in.

Note: You have to be careful about selecting a friend or group to work with. You want fun, productive, and motivated people who get things done *and* have fun. When you find people like that, it's a great way to get things done while having fun along the way.

7. Relax. Is your task something that you can relax while doing? Clear your mind and just enjoy what you are doing. Take deep breaths, stay hydrated, and enjoy!

8. Take frequent breaks. It's a good idea to set a timeframe to work on a task. Nobody wants to sit and reply to emails for four hours back-to-back. But if you break it down into 30-minute intervals, it'll be much more comfortable. Set your alarm or a timer, and have a break every so often so that you keep energized & focused on what you have to do.

Category #2: Concentration Tasks – These tasks require critical thinking and concentration, i.e., writing a report/book, studying, coding, reading, drawing, comparing, planning, assessing, etc. Here are some excellent ways to make them more engaging:

1. Put on soothing music without lyrics. This tip is similar to the music one mentioned earlier but with one significant change – the songs you play should not have lyrics. The reason behind it is that the words in a song can distract you. Because these activities demand 100% focus, make sure there are no lyrics. This is nothing new. Students usually put on soothing music in the background while studying. It not only helps them relax and feel good but also increases their focus. It can be applied to any concentration-heavy activity and make it an overall better experience.

2. Work together with a friend or a group. Two or more friends are always more fun than working alone. This is true even for concentration activities. There are multiple benefits. When you see your friends getting things done, it'll motivate you to do the same. You can joke around when you get tired. You can even help each other out if someone gets stuck with a problem. Make sure that you select productive people to work with and you'd get so much done while having a ball.

3. Try to do the task in a new way. Novelty can make even the most tedious of tasks into a fun one. You get bored because you have done a task many times before. There is nothing new to hold your interest. That leads to boredom. So, challenge yourself to come up with novel ways to do the work. While you cannot change the inherent boring nature of the task, you can definitely make it a lot more interesting by adding some variety to it. So, experiment, change, modify. Play around with it.

4. "Beat-the-clock" challenge. Here's another way to make boring activities more enjoyable. Find out how much time it usually takes to finish a task and then try to beat the clock. Once you do that, try to beat your previous best time. Essentially, you are competing with yourself. It makes work more exciting and engaging. Challenges tend to bring out the best in people, and we are using them to increase engagement and performance.

5. Try to do the best work you possibly can. Here's another way to spice up a boring activity. Instead of doing your work as per usual, try to do the best possible job that you can. For instance, if you are writing an email, try to make it the best email you have ever written. It is very engaging to push the boundaries of how well you can do a task. Undoubtedly, it will also increase the quality of your work significantly. You may start receiving appreciation from others for the quality of your work. But little do they know that you are doing it for a personal reason; it helps you get more engaged with your work.

This technique not only makes the work more interesting, but the higher quality of your output will benefit your company or customers. It's a win-win for everyone.

6. Set a reward for yourself after you finish the work. Set up a condition where you reward yourself when you meet a particular benchmark or result. For instance, tell yourself: if I read this specific number of pages today, I will reward myself with my favorite TV shows. The promise of a reward will keep you engaged with the task. (Upcoming chapters cover *setting rewards* in more detail.)

Boredom is a very real issue. I am sure there are more ways to make tasks more enjoyable. But these are some of the ones that I personally use and recommend to my clients. I hope they help you to make mundane activities a bit more fun & engaging.

> *"The key to success is not through achievement but through enthusiasm."* – **Malcolm Forbes**, American entrepreneur, and publisher of Forbes magazine.

Summary

- If you find your work boring, then it's easy for procrastination to creep in.

- It is possible to make even the most mundane of activities more fun.

- Use the guidelines above to make tasks more engaging.

- When you start having fun with work, it almost always leads to better productivity and results.

40. Apply The "W.I.F.M." Principle

The Problem

Deep down in your heart, you do know the benefits of doing that work on which you are procrastinating. You understand that the reading you've been postponing will help you secure good grades; you are well aware that that skill you are not learning now will help you enable more income; you admit that that yoga you are pushing to another time will make you healthier and allow you to live longer. These are outcomes you desire - then why are you not doing these things? You may want to list many plausible reasons, but they can all be summarized and are best explained in the dichotomy between instant gratification and delayed gratification.

Instant gratification is the desire to experience pleasure or fulfillment at once. Basically, you want something and you want it now. On the other hand, delayed gratification is the act of resisting an impulse to take an immediately available reward in the hope of obtaining more-valued compensation in the future.

Our brains are conditioned to always seek pleasure rather than excruciating work, and you know what? The brain wants to have fun now! Since that is a default nature of the brain, it becomes hard to fight immediate gratification.

That is why we are taking a different approach: why not incorporate fun into whatever boring work you have to do.

The Procrastination Solution

Let me introduce you to the concept of W.I.I.F.M. – What's in it for me. People tend to be a lot more productive when there is a promise of a reward at the end. It is wise to set up a reward system, where you get to reward yourself when you meet a particular benchmark or result. And what that reward should be is something fun and pleasurable. For instance, you tell yourself: if I read a specific number of pages today, I will reward myself with my favorite TV show. The thing is, if you don't attain that particular benchmark, you do not give yourself that reward. This system works even better if you have an *accountability partner* (as discussed in section I) and you put the reward in their care. If you don't reach the target, the person does not release it to you. For instance, if the TV show is to be aired on Netflix, make the person change your password and keep the password to themselves.

You can use high dopamine activities as a reward for completing difficult work. This is precisely what I do myself. To give you an example, for every finished hour of low dopamine work, I reward myself with 15 minutes of high dopamine activity at the end of the day. That means for every 8 hours of low dopamine work, I allow myself 2 hours of high dopamine activities. Of course, these are my ratios. You can tweak them to your liking.

It's important to note that if something is damaging to your health, then you don't want to treat that behavior as a reward. Instead, find something different that is not harmful in any way. If you are wondering what my guilty pleasure is – it's the internet. I can easily get lost in there for hours without doing anything else. That's why I have this system. It's so I can control my addiction. But make no mistake, even with this system, I plan days where I abstain from all dopamine activities completely.

The reward system is based on the psychological principle of pain & pleasure and is proven to increase productivity when applied correctly.

"For every disciplined effort, there are multiple rewards." – **Jim Rohn**, American author, speaker, and entrepreneur.

Summary

- Instant gratification is a common reason behind the habit of procrastination.

- A good counter is to set up a reward system where you get to reward yourself when you meet a particular benchmark or result.

- Make sure the reward is something you greatly desire.

- If it is damaging to your well-being, you don't want to treat it as a reward.

41. The Bright Side Of Challenges

The Problem

How often do you find your work absolutely and totally boring? Do you wish you could be doing something else?

You are not alone. A global poll conducted by Gallup concluded that only 15% of the world's full-time workers are fully engaged at work. An incredible 85% of people are dissatisfied with their jobs.

Link:
https://news.gallup.com/opinion/chairman/212045/world-broken-workplace.aspx

Even if you do like your job, there are usually some parts of it that you like and some parts that you will totally dislike. And boredom is one of the major reasons behind disliking parts of your job. The truth is; some tasks are just plain dull. They are bland. And it's so hard to feel passionate about doing something monotonous. It usually leads to procrastination.

The Procrastination Solution

The solution is to make your work more interesting. That's right. There are ways to turn even the most tedious tasks into something engaging. Let's go over some of them:

Solution #1 – Add a bit of competition. Competition fires up the brain and focuses your full attention. We can use this to spice up a monotonous task. Try this. Challenge a friend or co-worker to see who gets the work done the quickest.

If you want, take it a step further and set a prize for the winner. It doesn't have to be grand. It can be anything from a free coffee to a movie ticket. Whatever you may like!

It's essential to keep the competition friendly. Please don't go overboard, or it may end up being counterproductive.

Solution #2 – Challenge yourself. Try to beat your previous time or quality. For example:

- Creating daily reports is usually monotonous. Challenge yourself to finish them in a record time.

- If you find your workout boring, switch it up. Add more weights, or do more reps, or take fewer breaks, etc.

- If you need to send an email to a client, instead of the usual text, challenge yourself to make it the most incredible email you have ever sent.

Solution #3 – Dig deeper. If you pay close attention, you'll find that even the most boring tasks have multiple layers. There are so many details that are not apparent on the initial scan. But when you pay close attention to a task and dig deeper, you'll find many things that you do like!

For instance, if you are a student and find a subject boring, challenge yourself to find three interesting things in every chapter. It can be unusual facts, or a novel way to apply the principles, etc. Every subject can be intriguing. You only need to actively search for the parts you like.

Once you uncover the parts that are interesting, have fun. Change them. Play with them. Test out different approaches. There are so many possibilities.

If you keep an open mind and use a bit of creativity, you can come up with ways to make any work interesting. Do that - and the procrastination will take care of itself.

"Your work is going to fill a large part of your life, and the only way to be truly satisfied is to do what you believe is great work. The only way to do great work is to love what you do." – **Steve Jobs**, co-founder of Apple.

Summary

● Recent studies show that most people don't like what they do.

● Monotony and boredom are common reasons behind procrastination.

● Use the three solutions mentioned above to make the tasks more engaging.

● By using a bit of creative thinking, you can find ways to make any work enjoyable.

42. Accolades And The Flow Of Performance

The Problem

Sometimes, boredom can cause a significant drop in motivation. If you cannot find the motivation to start a new venture or just aren't feeling motivated enough to study, it can be a major roadblock between you and your goals.

For some people, a lack of motivation might be a small hindrance. For others, it could be something that they have been struggling with for years. The good news is that it can be overcome.

The key to dealing with low motivation is the way you handle it. While you'll come across several motivation strategies in the book, the next strategy is one of the simplest & effective you will find.

The Procrastination Solution

Sometimes you are able to overcome procrastination, right? Sometimes you power through and get the work done. We should try to reinforce this behavior.

Every time you overcome procrastination, follow through and get something done, give yourself a reward. Rewarding a behavior makes it stronger.

According to a research paper published by Gaby Judah, Benjamin Gardner & colleagues, a study with a total sample size of 118 participants concluded that pleasure (from rewards) could definitely help in habit formation.

Link to the article:
https://bmcpsychology.biomedcentral.com/articles/10.1186/s40359-018-0270-z

The rewards don't have to be extravagant. Even smaller rewards have the power to reinforce any good behavior. One of the simplest ways to reward yourself is using self-praise.

It goes like this. When you catch yourself doing the right thing (even a small action), give yourself some well-deserved praise such as 'Good job, (your name)!'

Using your name in the praise makes it much more personal. According to the field of psychology, a person's name is the most important word for them. Using your name in the compliment makes it penetrate deeper into your mind.

Give yourself compliments freely. Acknowledge every right action, no matter how small it might be. You did something right. Don't just push it aside as if it's nothing. Take the time to congratulate yourself for what you did.

You can even go one step further and keep a list of the times you beat procrastination. The power of the written word is astounding.

According to research done by Anne Mangen at the University of Stavanger, writing by hand strengthens the learning process. When typing on a keyboard or touch screen, this process may be impaired.

"*Writing by hand (pen and paper) strengthens the learning process. When we type on a keyboard or touch screen, this process may be impaired. Neurophysiologists have conducted a research which confirms the significance of these differences.*"

"While handwriting, our brain receives feedback from our motor actions, together with the sensation of touching a pen and *paper. This kind of feedback is very different from the one we receive when touching and typing on a keyboard."*

Make sure you use a pen and paper while doing this exercise.

When you write something down, you create a permanent reminder of that event. Whenever you'd look at your list, it will remind you of all those times you beat procrastination and got things done. As with verbal self-praise, this list will help create new neural pathways in the brain. Over time, it will make "taking action" your default mode of functioning.

"Praise, like sunlight, helps all things to grow" – **Croft M. Pentz**, Author.

Summary

● Boredom can cause a significant drop in motivation.

● One of the best ways to increase motivation is to reward yourself after successfully taking action.

● Even simple rewards like self-praise have the power to reinforce good behavior.

● You can even go a step further and keep a written list of the times you beat procrastination.

● Rewards help create new neural pathways in the brain. Over time, it can make "taking action" your default behavior.

43. The Element Of Time

The Problem

When you have a number of boring tasks to complete, it's not that you don't do anything at all. You still do. However, only the extremely important ones, like an assignment that has a deadline or an exam you got to write tomorrow. When this happens, you have no choice but to do that work.

However, in a case where the work has no deadline, like freelance or volunteering work, these don't seem to have an end, and often you don't get to do them at all. You end up delaying those tasks repeatedly.

The Procrastination Solution

A great strategy to overcome this situation is to manually set-up a deadline. It's quite effective for combating boredom-induced procrastination.

Having a deadline will do several positive things:

a) It will put positive pressure on you to take action, making sure you are not taking things too casually or acting lazy. It will make you much more efficient.

b) A deadline will allow you to measure your progress. For example, suppose you are writing your book and your plan is to finish two chapters in fifteen days (deadline). If you have not been able to complete your first chapter for eight days, it will become clear that your progress is slow. You will be forced to check where you are slipping and what you should do to get back on track.

c) It will make your goals feel real and subsequently increase your motivation. For instance, if your goal is to buy a new car, Toyota Camry, which of the following plans feel more real and motivating—

1) I will buy a Toyota Camry...

2) I will buy Toyota Camry within the next six months.

The first one has no definite end date, so it doesn't appear too inspiring. We think, *"someday it will happen. I don't know when."* In contrast, the second option feels much more tangible and real. You have a time frame. It will be done within six months. It has a definite end. You can see closure, and that makes it inspiring and motivating.

Some people are afraid that they will not be performing optimally under the pressure of an approaching deadline. That can happen, but rarely. Most of us become more productive the closer we are to the deadline.

Deadlines increase your focus. You will cut down any unnecessary activities that don't support you in moving toward your objective. A good analogy would be a race car that removes all its non-aerodynamic parts, which might slow it down; you'll prioritize only what is important. There will be a sense of urgency in you that will make you put in double the effort to get it done.

Another benefit is that the pressure will make you realize how productive you can be. You'll get to know the limits of how much you can get done. Some people believe they are too indecisive and passive. Such people are genuinely surprised to find how hard they can work under the pressure of an approaching deadline.

In the year 1908, psychologists Robert M. Yerkes and John Dillingham Dodson put forth the relationship between performance and pressure (from deadlines). It is called **Yerkes-Dodson law**. It states that work performance increases with increased pressure. But only up to a point. Too much or too low pressure can have adverse effects on performance.

The right amount of pressure can result in optimal performance. That is why we need to create the right deadlines.

How to Set Effective Deadlines?

A comprehensive study done at MIT by Dan Ariely on the effectiveness of a deadline pointed out the following:

1. External deadlines are more effective than self-imposed deadlines. For instance, a deadline given by your manager would be more effective than the deadline you put on yourself. Try to think of ways to put external deadlines on yourself.

2. If a person is a habitual procrastinator and they are aware of it, then a self-imposed deadline is a reasonably effective option to cope up with it.

3. Evenly-spaced deadlines tend to the most effective for improving productivity. Try to keep the amount of time between deadlines constant. For instance, if you have to complete three different tasks in a month, try to put equal distance between deadlines – let's say, a ten-day deadline for the first task, ten-day for the second, and ten for the third.

If you have four tasks to complete in a month, give yourself a week for each one. Try to keep the same distance between deadlines.

Link to the study:
https://erationality.media.mit.edu/papers/dan/eRational/Dynamic%20preferences/deadlines.pdf

Deadlines make you alert, focused, and motivated, which are all very beneficial for overcoming boredom. For that reason, adding a time-limit to work is almost always a good idea. You tend to work diligently and follow-through until the task is finished.

Make sure to add a deadline to every task or project you work on.

> "*The ultimate inspiration is the deadline.*" – **Nolan Bushnell**, American businessman and the co-founder of Atari.

Summary

• Having a deadline is critically important for overcoming boredom-induced procrastination.

• It puts positive pressure on you to take action, making sure you are not taking things too casually or acting lazy.

• External deadlines are more effective than self-imposed deadlines.

• Evenly-spaced deadlines tend to the most effective kind for improving productivity.

44. The Uncertain Agreement

The Problem

Do you often find it hard to complete boring tasks on your to-do list? Do you set out with your hopes up, only to realise you have not met your initial expectations?

Fortunately, there are some simple hacks that have proven to help many people beat their procrastination demons. Of course, what works for one person doesn't always work for another, but these behavioural changes are worth a try. It could be the one hack you've been looking for to help you get all your tasks in order and complete them in time — or even ahead of time!

The Procrastination Solution

Here's a unique strategy to overcome boredom-induced procrastination: a commitment device.

If you want to commit to something fully, raise the stakes. Risk something valuable, like $100 or more unless you deliver what you've promised.

But there's a catch. Let's take the a $100 commitment device as an example. It's not enough to make a promise that if you don't complete your work by the due date that you will pay someone $100. No, the commitment must be made beforehand, at the time when you're all fired up and ready to commit to being productive.

A Commitment Device in Action

Here's how it works. Let's say you've got a work or school assignment due late next week, but you're determined to get it done over the weekend. Doing so will give you a few more days to refine your ideas and make any changes that occur to you, rather than rushing off the assignment at the last minute.

Let's say you're so committed to getting this done that you're willing to put $100 on the line. Here's what you need to do. Put $100 in an envelope and give it to someone you trust under strict instructions that they are only to return it to you if you can prove that you have completed the work you set out to do by the end of the weekend. On the front of the envelope, write down exactly should happen to the $100 if you don't meet your goal.

This backup plan can't be anything that's going to make you feel good. You can't promise to donate the $100 to your favourite charity, because that could be all the impetus your procrastinating brain needs to shirk your work over the weekend. Donating $100 to your favourite charity is a good thing, right? No, that just won't work. The backup plan has to involve doing something with that $100 that would be almost physically painful for you.

Perhaps it will be sent as a donation in your name to your least favourite political party or an organisation you truly despise. Perhaps it will be burnt to nothing right in front of your eyes. The mental image of what will happen to your money if you don't follow through with your plan should be all the impetus you need to get moving.

Although such a strategy may seem hard to employ, the truth is that it works wonders. Betting is used as a means of forcing yourself to stay true to your end goal. Unless such risks are taken, you do not feel intimidated by the time frame. When you add monetary loss to the game — along with the hopefully bad image of what will happen to your money if you don't do what you say you're going to do –things change, and your mindset does too.

Of course, you can vary this type of commitment device in any way that works for you. It doesn't have to be money. Maybe you give your favourite item of clothing to a friend under strict instructions that it gets jumped straight into the nearest charity bin if you don't meet your goal. Whatever commitment device you choose, it has to be something that you set up in advance and that only doesn't happen if you don't do what you say you're going to do. It can't be something that you promise to do later. You must be held accountable, and the consequence must be completely in place before you begin.

Being on time is of the essence, especially when it comes to people leading busy lives. Instead of playing with the odds, you may use commitment devices to your benefit. When the clock is ticking, and you really must finish your project on time, give this uncommon strategy a try.

"The fear of loss is greater than the desire for gain." – **Zig Ziglar**, American author and speaker.

Summary

- Raising the stakes increases your commitment to getting a task done.

- For instance, give someone $100 and tell them to give it back to you only when you finish a specific task in a fixed time period.

- Although such a strategy may seem hard to employ, the truth is that it works wonders.

- The fear of loss is one of the strongest motivating factors in the human psyche. Commitment devices allow us to use it for our benefit.

45. Seek To Eliminate Complexity

The Problem

More often than not, we find ourselves bored because the task we have appears to be too complex. We feel overwhelmed and confused. We hesitate to get started because we're not sure how to go about it.

The real cause behind this kind of procrastination is not the boredom itself. It's the negative feeling of being overwhelmed. To avoid feeling bad, we tend to divert our attention to some other fun activities like watching movies and browsing social media. We know that our work is important and must be done, but it's too complicated, and we don't want to feel uncomfortable.

The Procrastination Solution

The way to handle this situation is to reduce the complexity of your work.

When the work is too complicated and confusing, here's what you should do:

1. Gather just enough information to get started.

2. Condense it down to simple, easy-to-follow action steps.

I call it a *blueprint plan*. It is simply an outline of the actual steps you would take.

Here is an example of a blueprint plan.

Suppose your goal is to get in shape. Your blueprint plan to get you started could be:

1st step - Join a gym

2nd step - Get familiar with exercises (hire a trainer if required)

3rd step - Start working out five times a week (or as needed)

4th step - Gain information about what to eat and what to avoid

5th step - Start eating healthy

6th step - Keep improving your workout and diet

And so on.

Another example:

If you want to improve your marketing:

1st step - Read at least two marketing books this month

2nd step - Understand your niche better (study competitors, do a survey, etc.)

3rd step - Contact and set up meetings with your marketing team

4th step - Try two different marketing strategies in the next thirty days

And so on.

It is miles better than what many people do - having no plan at all. Please don't do this without any plan. Create a general frame of what you should do.

I am calling it *general* because it's a fresh and tentative plan that should help you get started initially. Later on, as you gain more experience and information, you should make changes in it accordingly and keep moving forward.

Having an initial blueprint plan will give you something, to begin with. It will reduce the initial complexity and allow you to take action.

And the best part is - it can be updated as you gain more ideas and greater experience. The flexibility to grow is a major strength of a blueprint plan. You don't have to wait for the "perfect plan." There will never be a perfect plan at the beginning.

Keep it simple. Just gather enough information to create a tentative step-by-step plan and start taking action. When you reduce the complexity of the work, it becomes much easier to get started.

> *"Simplicity is one of my mantras. You have to work hard to get your thinking clean to make it simple. But it's well worth it in the end because once you get there, you can move mountains."* –
> **Steve Jobs**, co-founder of Apple.

Summary

- Sometimes, we find ourselves bored because the task is too complicated and confusing.

- Gather just enough information to get started and condense it down to simple, easy-to-follow action steps. That's your blueprint plan.

- At this point, just start taking action. You can make changes to the plan as you gain more experience and information.

46. The Validity Of Boredom Management

The Problem

Everyone experiences boredom. We all get bored sometimes during our day. According to a recent survey, 63% of participants among 3867 adults report experiencing boredom at least once a day, across the ten-day sampling period.

Link to survey:
https://pubmed.ncbi.nlm.nih.gov/27775405/

Boredom feels like mental tiredness and commonly stems from a lack of novelty & interest in the task at hand. Any activity that is predictable and provides little stimulation feels boring.

And here's the real kicker - we all have a few boring tasks that must be completed. Things like doing exercise, filing taxes, studying a subject you don't like, and doing house chores may feel incredibly dull. So we look for ways to avoid them.

Some activities can be easily avoided, but some are crucial. But even then, we cannot make ourselves get up and do them because of their boring nature.

So, how do we handle tasks such as these?

The Procrastination Solution

Here's the secret to getting around boring activities: *Don't resist it.*

It's okay to be bored sometimes. It's fine. We have been conditioned to avoid boredom at all costs. But being bored is not a bad thing. There are actually some benefits of boredom.

Boredom provides a balance. Think about it. Being bored makes you appreciate the fun times. If you never experience boredom, then having fun will lose its meaning. According to the *Law of Familiarity* in psychology, when we experience something all the time, we start to lose interest in it. It becomes "too familiar."

For instance, watching one good movie a couple of times can be fun, but watching it ten times back-to-back would be unbearable.

Here's another one. Most people have a sweet tooth. They love ice-creams, chocolates, and other wonderful sweets. But what if sweet was the only taste there was. It would get boring real quick. Bitter, salty, and other flavors provide balance and meaning to the sweetness.

The same applies to having fun.

Having fun all the time is not as wonderful as we think. It must be balanced with a few moments of boredom. It makes having fun a richer experience. If we never experience boredom, the fun will lose its meaning.

So, don't resist boring activities. Welcome boredom. It's okay to be bored sometimes. In fact, it is required for a richer life experience.

Don't avoid boring activities like:

- Answering emails
- Waiting in a line
- Exercise
- Buying groceries
- Studying
- Cleaning up the house

Remember, being bored sometimes is fine. Do the work anyway. Don't let the boredom stop you. Good and bad. Boring and fun. Sweet and sour. They are all part of life. They complete each other.

> *"Even a happy life cannot be without a measure of darkness, and the word happy would lose its meaning if it were not balanced by sadness. It is far better to take things as they come along with patience and equanimity."* - **Carl Jung,** founder of analytical psychology.

Side note: If you feel bored ALL the time, then you might need to take a deep, hard look at the choices you have made. If you are constantly bored at your job, find out what interests you and switch jobs to that field. If you are a student and don't like your current subjects, change them to the ones you find fascinating. If you are an entrepreneur and feel bored all the time, start a new venture in a field that captures your interest. You'll become more joyful and engaged.

Changes like these might not be a walk in the park, but they are well worth the effort. Find out what interests you, and be on the lookout for an opportunity. Switch over as soon as you see one. Life is just too short to slog away doing things that *constantly* bore you out of your mind. You deserve better.

Summary:

- Don't try to avoid boring activities. It's *okay* to be bored sometimes. Boredom creates a balance and lets you appreciate the fun times.

Section IV
What To Do When You Get Distracted

Are you easily distracted? Does your concentration break easily? If you are having trouble with focusing on the tasks at hand, it can be deeply problematic.

For instance, you are working on a report, but your mind is distracted the whole time, and it's making the task unnecessarily difficult. Or, suppose you are working from home but are getting distracted constantly by other people.

Distractions are a major roadblock to productivity. Even a small interruption can result in a lot of wasted time. Fortunately, there are ways to deal with it.

In this section, we are going to cover some practical and immediately applicable methods to fend off distractions and get stuff done.

47. The Restoration Of Willpower Reserves

The Problem

Distractions are detrimental to your productivity. A few times in this book, it is recommended that you maintain your focus and push yourself to take action. While it can be a sound strategy, sometimes 'pushing yourself' may not be enough to overcome distractions. Maybe you cannot force yourself that much.

In that case, improving your willpower will be the answer to overcoming distractions.

The Procrastination Solution

Many people think self-discipline is the most important trait for being productive. I beg to differ. I believe if you have enough willpower, you will be able to maintain a disciplined life easily. Think of willpower as fuel for discipline. You won't be able to maintain it if your willpower is lacking.

In her excellent book *Maximum Willpower*, Dr. Kelly McGonigal says willpower is like a muscle. It gets exhausted with use. The more willpower requiring activities we do, the lesser our willpower reserves have. When it reaches a very low level, it becomes very difficult to fight with excuses and procrastination.

Thankfully, there are ways to recharge and even strengthen your willpower. The easiest and the most effective way to increase your willpower is to meditate for 10 minutes every day.

Italian neuroscientists Barbara Tomasino and Franco Fabbro examined the brain scans of participants after an eight-week long mindfulness meditation practice. They found increased activity in the dorsolateral prefrontal cortex (PFC) area of the brain, which is responsible for focus and willpower.

Link to research:
https://pubmed.ncbi.nlm.nih.gov/26720411/

I believe this easy breathing exercise is a MUST for everyone who aspires to be more productive. Do meditation daily, and within a month, you will start noticing increased willpower and many other benefits like increased concentration, focus, emotional balance, happiness, and reduced stress & negative thoughts.

Once you start seeing its benefits, you will be surprised why someone didn't tell you about it earlier.

It's important to note that the core practice of meditation has no attachment to any religion. At its very core, meditation is about focusing on your breath for a short period of time. We are not concerned with spirituality here.

While meditation can be a powerful spiritual practice, you always have the option of not attaching it to religion and still get the practical, daily life benefits of increased willpower and discipline. It's very easy to do and takes only 10 minutes a day to get the full benefits.

How to Meditate?

1. Set an alarm for 10 minutes.

2. Sit comfortably on a chair, keeping your back relaxed & upright. Use a cushion if you need to.

3. Close your eyes and start noticing your breath coming in and out. Notice everything about it: when it enters your nostrils to when it goes in your diaphragm, the movement of your stomach going up and down, etc.

Eventually, your mind will start thinking about something. You'll lose focus on your breath and start dwelling on the thought itself. That's okay.

4. Whenever you catch yourself focusing on your thoughts instead of being aware of your breath, gently and calmly shift your focus back to your breath.

5. Soon, you will lose your focus again and get lost in thoughts. Relax, and simply shift your focus to your breath again.

6. Keep doing this for 10 minutes till your alarm rings.

Note: Don't force yourself to keep your mind empty all the time. The mind will think, and that's what we want. Actually, the willpower gets stronger when you keep shifting your focus from your thoughts to your breath. This 'to-and-from' of awareness is what strengthens your willpower. It's like a gym for the mind.

This simple exercise will increase your willpower levels to astronomical levels. Its effectiveness is unmatched. I would even confess that I would not be able to finish my first book if it wasn't for meditation. Our daily life has become so demanding that we end up having a very low reserve of willpower.

This simple exercise is the answer. It will replenish the lost supply of willpower and even increase its capacity. It is 'Highly recommended'.

"Our performance depends on so many factors, out of which, only some we can control. What I can surely control is my mind and what I mentally bring to the starting line." – **Bonnie Blair**, six-time Olympic medal winner in speed skating.

Summary

- If you get distracted easily, then your willpower needs improvement.

- Meditation is an excellent exercise to strengthen willpower.

- Use the guidelines mentioned above to practice meditation daily for 5-10 minutes.

- According to recent studies, meditation provides benefits like increased concentration, focus, emotional balance, and reduced stress.

48. Noncompliance Is Essential

The Problem

Frequent requests from others can easily distract you from work. Perhaps your boss has a habit of asking you to work on and finish projects on very short timelines. Or perhaps you have neighbors who ask for your help with gardening or moving stuff. Or maybe you have a friend who asks for your help quite often with school work - listening to him practice speeches, reviewing his written work, or getting help with difficult problems.

Too many requests from other people can have you pretty much occupied and leave you with no time on your hands to handle things on your own 'to-do' list, and you end up procrastinating.

We're asked for our support throughout the day - people requesting your time, energy, attention, and advice. It happens everywhere - at work, home, and even on the street with complete strangers. While giving and taking is an integral part of life, saying "yes" every time someone needs your help - at the expense of your own priorities - can drain you of energy and even happiness.

The Procrastination Solution

The next time someone comes up with a request, and it's distracting you away from work, you have a right to say 'no'. Saying 'no' to constant requests from other people really goes a long way in overcoming procrastination.

Here's what saying 'no' will give back to you:

• **More time and energy**: The fact that you are now in conscious control will save you a lot of time and energy.

- **More confidence**: Saying 'no' to others can often amount to saying 'yes' to yourself. This is a back-handed 'I love you' to the most important person in your life - you. Please take it as a compliment and feel good about it.

- **More control**: Saying 'no' means you are the decision-maker and do whatever you want.

- **More respect**: You'll get more respect from people when you show them your clear, no-discussion limits.

- **More fun**: Yes, life is to be enjoyed. When you stop working for others, you start working for yourself and start fitting in the fun.

Here are some things to keep in mind when declining requests:

1. Try to be polite when refusing requests. There is a fine line between being confident and being rude. Our goal is to be calm and concise during the interaction.

2. Explain the reason behind your refusal to the person making the request. Many times, people have no idea how busy you really are. Once they get to know about your jam-packed schedule, they walk away with no hard feelings. Here are a few examples:

"I am afraid I can't because…"
"I prefer not to because…"
"I would rather not as…"

When you are polite and explain the reason behind your response, the other person does not feel disrespected. It allows them to walk away while keeping the relationship intact.

3. Be confident. Don't ask for more time to consider unless you really need it. If you do ask for more time, they will come back later. Will you ask for more time again? Eventually, you'll have to say "yes" or "no."

So, it'd be better to make a decision on the first instance and save time for both of you. Be confident and respect your decision. If you are busy, let them know.

4. Mind your non-verbal communication. Your body language and voice tone plays an important role in the interaction. If you speak in a timid voice and don't make eye contact, the other person will not take your words seriously and might push against your 'no'.

You have to show you're serious by displaying confident non-verbal communication. During the conversation, speak in a firm voice tone and make steady eye contact. Using your voice and eyes this way will amplify the effects of your words. The other person will get the message clearly.

> "It is only by saying no that you can concentrate on things that are really important." – **Steve Jobs**, co-founder of Apple.

When you decline a request in the manner described above, you have communicated your intentions clearly and it gives other people a chance to understand your situation. They would respect your honesty and walk away with no hard feelings.

Summary

• Constant requests from other people can leave you with no time to handle things on your to-do list.

• Use the guidelines above to communicate your intentions clearly and respectfully.

- Saying 'no' to constant requests from other people really goes a long way to be more productive.

49. Identify The Dimensions Of Your Attention Span

The Problem

Do you have trouble maintaining focus on the task at hand?

For instance, you have a critical meeting at work but your mind is wandering the whole time, causing you to miss critical information or have an inability to come up with new ideas. Or, suppose you are trying to do your homework but cannot seem to find the energy or focus to get it done.

Research conducted by psychologists Matthew A. Killingsworth and Daniel T. Gilbert of Harvard University says that people spend around 47% of the time wondering about what isn't happening in the present moment.

Link to research:
https://news.harvard.edu/gazette/story/2010/11/wandering-mind-not-a-happy-mind/

Fortunately, there are some good ways to improve your concentration, focus, and creativity.

The Procrastination Solution

Here's a solution that has worked well for many of my clients - be familiar with your peak performance time and schedule work accordingly.

Let me explain. Some people tend to have more energy in the morning, while others do their best work at night. Whatever your preferred time to work is, you need to schedule your day so that the majority of your most important work falls during the time of the day when you can perform your best.

For example, I am a morning person. I tend to do my best in the morning. I can also work in the afternoon and night, but the quality & quantity of my morning work is far superior.

The same thing goes for our energy levels. It tends to fluctuate during the course of the day. Some people feel more energetic in the morning and others during the day or late at night... Plan your day around it. Try working at different times of the day to find your own preferred time period in which you feel most energetic, and schedule your work at that time.

This single step will increase your productivity immensely.

Bonus tip: As stated in earlier sections, when you take care of your health, emotions, influences, etc., you will feel energetic most of the time during the day. In other words, your "peak performance time" window will get larger.

A bigger "peak performance" window means you would do your best work for longer periods of time.

> *"It is impossible to produce superior performance unless you do something very different."* – **John Templeton**, investor, banker, fund manager, and philanthropist.

Summary

- Lack of concentration and focus is a universal cause of procrastination.

- Every person has a preferred time to work during which they are at their best.

- A good strategy is to find your peak performance time and schedule work accordingly.

- It will result in a noticeable increase in your productivity.

50. Build Shelter Against Chaos

The Problem

Procrastination is known to feed off our distractions. Whenever novel and brain-stimulating distractions are available at your fingertips — such as funny cat videos, scrolling through social media, video games – well, it's hard to resist their temptation.

Usually, these kinds of distractions are more enjoyable and exciting than our work — and therefore, they are more appealing. Just one quick glance at your e-mail inbox or latest posts by friends, and before you realize, you're lost in an internet vortex and have lost an hour that could have been spent more productively. Repeat this several times a day, and you can see how much focus and productivity you end up losing.

Even worse, every time we get distracted, it takes an average of 25 minutes to regain our full focus on the task that we were working on. This is called attention residue, which means that a portion of your attention is left behind on the previous task that you were involved with.

The Procrastination Solution

The answer is to take care of distractions before we start working on our priority tasks. We need to create a distraction-free environment that allows us to focus completely on work for a long period of time. It enables us to finally overcome procrastinating and boost productivity.

Here's what you should do. Create a period of time in your day when you're free of all distractions. This does a lot towards fighting procrastination as outside "noise" can disrupt your focus and, subsequently, the work you get done.

Point out all the distractions you typically experience in your day and take steps to make sure they can't affect you during your "no-distraction" period. Websites, apps, devices, people, whatever it might be.

1. Put off all notifications on your phone and PC.

2. Keep your phone away or on airplane mode.

3. Close your social media and e-mail notifications.

4. Tell your friends and family not to disturb you during this period.

5. Work in a quiet and comfortable environment.

Example #1 – Your phone is probably the biggest source of distraction. Constant notifications, calls, messages, and apps immediately highjack your attention and can easily distract you for hours. If your phone is in your immediate workspace, you probably wouldn't be able to concentrate on work. Put it on silent mode and keep it outside your room or in a drawer.

Just the absence of your phone can boost your productivity. When you don't have access to myriads of apps and notifications on your phone, you'll be free to focus on important things like work, exercise, studies, spending time with family, reconnecting with old friends. There are so many wonderful things out there that are often ignored because we are preoccupied with the trivial digital stuff which fills our lives.

Example #2 – Tell your friends and family about your work period. Say you will get back to them after your work session is over. They would understand and respect your schedule because they love you and want to see you do well.

Once you manage to get your phone and social circle to not distract you, it's a major step towards becoming more productive. These two are usually the biggest sources of distraction for most people. The rest of the distractions are relatively easier to manage.

Do your best to create a period of time in your day when you're free from all distractions. You'll be able to work with full focus and concentration.

So, isolate yourself. Lock-in. Focus. And get the job done!

> *"By prevailing over all obstacles and distractions, one may unfailingly arrive at their chosen goal or destination"* –
> **Christopher Columbus**, Italian explorer and navigator who opened the way to colonization of America.

Summary

- Distractions are one of the most common causes of procrastination.

- The solution is to take care of distractions ahead of time.

- Set a period of time in your day when you're free from all distractions.

- Silence all notifications, keep your phone away and lock your room, so no one can disturb you.

- Shut out all distractions. Lock-in. Focus. And get the job done!

51. The Truth Behind Efficiency In A Distracted World

The Problem

As our society is progressing, we are constantly trying to make things easier, shorter & faster. The advancement in technology brought a new shift in our behavior. We have developed a deep fondness for quick fixes or magic pills.

Look at the commercials on TV today- "six-minute abs" or "the diet pill."

People are using drugs & alcohol to "feel good." In business, people are chasing "get-rich-fast" schemes. In sports, athletes are getting caught using enhancements.

We want to feel good and successful, and we want it RIGHT NOW!

I believe there's a reason behind it. From birth, a child's mind is bombarded with instant gratification from all angles. Parents turn on the TV so the kids can watch cartoons and don't annoy them with requests to play. From a very young age, we are exposed to advertisements, television, video games, fast food, and social media.

All of these are designed to make you feel good in short bursts. Once the "good feelings" run out, you come back for more. Thus, becoming addicted to instant gratification.

There are several things wrong with instant gratification. To start, you lose good feelings the moment "stimulation" ends. For instance, if you are playing a video game and feel really good, just watch how it feels when you turn it off.

It's over, and you go back to feeling lousy the moment you return to the real world. This fleeting nature of happiness makes you come back for more. It's like being on drugs. You want more and more and more...

Second, it distracts you from what really matters in the long term. Some people who intend to lose weight eat ice-cream because it feels good at the moment. People go and watch movies instead of spending time together and having a meaningful conversation. People prefer to watch daily soap operas & filling their minds with drama instead of reading and learning.

We want a short-cut to happiness and don't really want to put in the effort.

And, it never works.

The Procrastination Solution

True happiness & fulfillment come after you WORK on your heart's calling. Whenever I ignore any important work and do something meaningless (i.e., watch TV) to divert my mind, I feel guilty. It's like a constant, almost undetectable shame. It makes the craving for instant gratification even stronger, leading to more internal pain and anxiety, which further intensifies the craving.

It's a negative cycle and something which you must break out of.

A study done by Fuschia M. Sirois & Natalia Tosti revealed the link between stress and instant gratification/procrastination.

A univariate analysis of 339 students revealed that procrastination is associated with high stress, low mindfulness, and poor perceived health.

Link to study:
https://link.springer.com/article/10.1007/s10942-012-0151-y

The first and the most effective way to break the instant-gratification habit is to realize that instant gratification can never make you happy. True happiness and satisfaction lie in TAKING ACTION towards your goals. When you move towards your heart's calling, you experience deep, long-lasting fulfillment.

Many people are afraid to take action. They fear being overwhelmed with work and challenges they may encounter.

In reality, nothing is further away from the truth.

Initially, you may resist doing your work, but I assure you, when you DO start, it will be the best feeling in the world. You will feel light. You will feel great. You will feel that this is THE most appropriate thing you could have done at this moment.

After you finish your work today, you will have a deep sense of satisfaction. You will laugh more. You will enjoy the simple pleasures of life which you would have ignored earlier. Little things will make you happy… because you are fulfilled inside. For today, the most important thing is done. You have finished your part.

> "The ability to delay gratification in the short term in order to enjoy the greater rewards in the future is the prerequisite of success." – **Maxwell Maltz**, American cosmetic surgeon and author.

Summary

Avoid seeking instant gratification. The good feelings are temporary and will disappear quickly. Instead, follow your heart's calling. Put your best effort into it. You will experience long-lasting, REAL happiness & satisfaction.

52. How To Avert Perpetual Disorientation

The Problem

Distractions are your number one enemy when it comes to keeping your focus. Some habits for instance, can induce procrastination.

If distractions have become a problem for you, here are quick ways to change your behavior so you can be more productive. An added benefit is that you'll feel more upbeat, less worried and stressed, and more confident about your reputation and effectiveness.

The Procrastination Solution

Distractions kill motivation. Here is what you do if you want to achieve your goals and get ahead in life:

Completely cut out everything that doesn't support you.

Don't eat any type of food that doesn't support you.

Don't look at any type of influence like television or media or celebrity gossip websites.

Do not play video games.

Do not watch movies.

Minimize alcohol consumption.

Minimize interactions with people who distract you from moving towards your goals.

Do not do anything that makes you waste your time.

When you set a goal, you make a commitment - it must be the single focus of your daily life.

If you want to be relaxed and have fun, please do not set a goal.

Setting a goal demands your complete attention, and if you are unwilling to give up all other leisure activities, don't set a goal.

The reason is there's no middle ground. Either you are fully committed to a single objective or not. If you mix both - committing to a goal AND being relaxed – it's a recipe for disaster.

You will neither be relaxed nor productive. You will be confused and worried all the time about what you should do and shouldn't do.

Decide what you want to do. If you want to relax and take things easy, do that. If you want to achieve something important to you, commit fully to it and cut-off all distractions.

If you choose to follow the latter, you will experience an unbelievable surge in your motivation and productivity.

"A distracted existence leads us to no goals." – **Johann Wolfgang von Goethe**, German poet, playwright, and novelist.

Summary

• Distractions are your number one enemy when it comes to productivity.

• A good way to manage distractions is to cut out everything that could hold you back from taking action.

- Setting a goal demands your complete attention, and if you are unwilling to give up all other leisure activities, don't set a goal.

- If you mix both - committing to a goal AND being relaxed – you will neither be relaxed nor productive. You will be confused and worried all the time about what you should do and shouldn't do.

53. The Unforeseen Ally

The Problem

On your way to success, one of the biggest distractions you would have to overcome is fear. It stops people from believing in themselves, dreaming big, and taking action.

Each one of us is afraid. We all have fears. But anyone who has become successful had to overcome their fears. There is no other way. If you don't take control of your fear, then fear will control you.

You must have the upper hand here. Fear will always BLOCK you from making progress in life. When you are taking a step ahead, it will ALWAYS be there to stop you. And it will become even stronger as you get closer to the finish line.

However, there is a way to make fear work in your favor.

The Procrastination Solution

One of the most powerful types of fear is the fear of loss. A person would do everything in their power to avoid loss. Even if there are more chances of good things happening. Think about it. Suppose if you have $100,000 in your bank account, and you get an opportunity to turn it into $200,000, but there is a 40% chance you would lose all of your money. Will you take that opportunity?

Most people would answer - "No."

Why is that?

According to the science of psychology, losing something is one of the scariest sensations we could ever feel. We will do more to avoid a loss than to gain something new. It's one of the major drives of human behavior. The need to prevent losses is hardwired into our brains.

But what if we could use this fear to push us forward instead of stopping us? Can you imagine how powerful it can be?

Using Fear in Your Favor

Here's how to use fear of loss to your advantage:

Step 1. Think about something that you are procrastinating on.

Step 2. Find a quiet & comfortable place (usually the bedroom).

Step 3. Close your eyes and imagine what would happen if you DON'T take action. What would you miss out on?

Step 4. Make it intense. Think about all the things you would lose if you don't take action – all your dreams, aspirations, passions, and the trust of other people... all gone. You may fail to tap into your potential and now live a subpar life... when you could have done so much more. You could have achieved so much for your family, for your friends, for your society. Think of all the people you could have helped... now they all suffer because you didn't take the right action... when you had the time.

Keep adding more intensity till it becomes unbearable to imagine.

Step 5. Open your eyes and make a promise to yourself that you would not let procrastination ruin your future. Write it down on a piece of paper.

This exercise takes around 10 minutes to complete. You'll experience a level of motivation you probably have never experienced before. You will be raring to go. There will be spring in your steps. You will end up blazing through the work effortlessly.

If you keep doing this exercise daily for around 10 minutes, it will create new pathways in the brain via neuroplasticity and make taking action your habit.

Could it get any better?

"You are what you do, not what you say you'll do" – **Carl Gustav Jung**, Swiss psychiatrist and founder of analytical psychology.

Summary

- One of the biggest roadblocks to productivity is fear. Especially fear of failure or loss.

- There are ways to switch things around. Use the exercise provided to make fear work in your favor.

- Do this exercise daily for about 10 minutes to rewire your brain for better productivity.

54. The Psychology Of Intrinsic Motivation

The Problem

We are taught that a high motivation level is one of the best ways to deal with distractions. But there is more to this story. There are different types of motivation.

If you are motivated by outside things, events, or other people, then that is called external motivation. The source of that motivation is external. Someone or something is motivating you to take action.

The issue with external motivation is that it doesn't last. As soon as you get separated from the source of your external motivation, you lose your enthusiasm. In order to achieve long-lasting motivation, we need to tap into intrinsic motivation.

When you choose to do something purely because you find it interesting, that's intrinsic motivation. You are not influenced by anyone or anything outside of yourself. Your drive comes from within yourself and propels you to take action.

There is a lot of power in intrinsic motivation. Unlike external motivation, it doesn't fade away. It is self-sustaining and can last a lifetime. Intrinsic motivation makes you seek out challenges and develop your skills & knowledge, even if the rewards are not immediately obtainable.

Link to a comprehensive study on the benefits of intrinsic motivation:
https://www.ncbi.nlm.nih.gov/pmc/articles/PMC5364176/

Your hobbies are a result of intrinsic motivation. No one is putting pressure on you to do crossword puzzles, or read a romance novel, or go mountain hiking. You pursue your hobbies because you want to. The best part is - your hobbies usually last a lifetime due to the nature of intrinsic motivation.

The Procrastination Solution

So how do we tap into the power of intrinsic motivation?

The solution is to go deep within and ask yourself, *"what do I want?"*

No! Say it louder!!!

"What do I REALLY, REALLY, REALLY want?"

To tap into the intrinsic motivation, get familiar with your deepest desires and then set those desires as goals to pursue. These goals should make you feel humbled at the thought of achieving them. Whenever you think about them, you should feel a shiver down your spine. You should feel crazy amounts of desire, excitement, and joy.

These are the kind of goals that trigger intrinsic motivation.

> *"80 percent of success is due to psychology—mindset, beliefs, and emotions—and only 20 percent is due to strategy—the specific steps needed to accomplish a result"* – **Anthony Robbins**, the premier leadership and performance expert.

When you set modest goals, your emotions will not be there. But when you set goals that make you feel excited, that's a major success in itself.

You'll give your 100% to obtain it because it's so compelling. You'll have an incredible drive.

Some of my clients ask me, *"Should I set smaller goals? I am not certain if I could achieve my bigger goals?"*

My answer - it's always better to shoot for the moon because even if you miss, you will land among the stars.

Take an example, which of the below results would be more desirable? You set a goal of making $10,000 in a year and reach it... Or...You set a goal of making $100,000 in a year but miss it by a little margin.

Of course, a little less than $100,000 is still better than $10,000!

The point here is, even if you miss a bigger goal, it will be better than obtaining a small goal. The size of your goals will determine the amount of success you will have in your life.

> *"The greatest fear for most of us isn't that our aim is too high and we miss it, but that it is too low and we reach it."* - **Michelangelo,** revered sculptor, painter, architect & poet of the Italian renaissance.

The solution is to tap into your desires and go for something you REALLY want. Set greater goals. Go for the ones which make you feel alive. Only then will you unlock your true inner drive. Only then will you conjure enough energy to succeed at the highest level. That's how you become the best version of yourself. That's how you become the person you were designed to be.

Get in touch with yourself. Be introspective and find out what you desire the most. It has to be something that means a lot to you. That is how you tap into intrinsic motivation.

It's important not to limit yourself when defining a goal. Nothing is off-limits in this process. Let it be as wild as it can get. If your craving for your goal is deep enough, it's worth going after. The more intense your desire, the more chance you have of succeeding.

That's it. If you follow the instructions above and create a goal that triggers your intrinsic motivation, it's a *major* win in itself. I would go as far as to say, selecting the right goal is the closest thing to a magic pill for productivity. It's a huge step in overcoming distractions and other self-defeating behaviors.

> *"You can motivate by fear, and you can motivate by reward. But both those methods are temporary. The only lasting thing is self-motivation."* – **Homer Rice**, Renowned American football player, coach, and athletics administrator.

Summary

- Motivation is considered one of the best ways to deal with distractions.

- There are two types of motivation – external and intrinsic. Unfortunately, external motivation doesn't last.

- We must tap into intrinsic motivation by asking ourselves, *"if money was no object, what would I want to do or be?"*

- If you follow the instructions above and create a goal that triggers your intrinsic motivation, it'll be a huge step in overcoming distractions and other self-defeating behaviors.

55. Weekly Performance Analysis Methodology

The Problem

Not knowing whether you are making progress or not is another common reason behind procrastination. Whenever we are unsure if what we are doing is working, then it can cause confusion, and confusion leads to getting distracted.

What we need is a way to track our progress. However, when we are caught up in our daily routine, moving from one task to another, tracking our progress is the last thing that comes into our mind.

The Procrastination Solution

Here's a solution: Conduct a weekly performance review. It's a simple process and doesn't take too long. The benefit of a weekly performance review is that you'll be able to track your progress, identify your strengths & weaknesses, and chart the future course of action.

You'll be able to evaluate your process and make adjustments. No need to wait for a year to review whether you're on track or not. Weekly performance reviews help you gain perspective, gather feedback, and make quick changes if needed, which is almost a requirement in today's competitive workplace.

Weekly Performance Review Guidelines

When conducting a weekly performance review, you'll have to evaluate four main areas:

Part #1 - Past performance: How was my previous week's performance? Check all parameters. What did I accomplish or didn't accomplish, and why?

Part #2 - Current status: What's my current progress compared to my end goal(s)? What are my loose ends? What's pending?

Part #3 - Future course of action: What should I do in the next seven days? Do I keep going like this or do I need to make adjustments?

Part #4 - Think outside the box: What else could I do to increase my productivity? Brainstorm new ideas.

These four areas cover all your major performance matrixes: Past performance, current status, pending tasks, the future course of action, and creative new solutions. Conducting a weekly performance review based on these parameters will allow you to obtain unprecedented levels of clarity to your progress. You'll know exactly what to focus on and accomplish in the next seven days. It will create a sense of urgency and guard your mind against distractions.

If you frequently think, *"I don't know where I am going, or am I on track?"* then a weekly performance review is the solution. It will highlight your strengths, pinpoint your weaknesses, reveal your position, and bring transparency to the whole process.

"It takes humility to seek feedback. It takes wisdom to understand it, analyze it, and appropriately act on it." **– Stephen Covey**, author of *The 7 Habits of Highly Effective People*.

Summary

• Whenever we are not sure if what we are doing is working, then it can cause confusion, and confusion leads to getting distracted.

- The solution is to conduct a weekly performance review. Use the 4-step method to bring unprecedented levels of clarity to your progress.

- It will highlight your strengths, pinpoint your weaknesses, reveal your position, and bring transparency to the whole process.

56. Monthly Performance Analysis Process

We have covered weekly performance reviews, but monthly performance reviews (MPR) are also worth mentioning. These are similar to the weekly ones but with few main differences.

Monthly performance reviews also highlight your strengths, weakness, current position, pending tasks, and future path of action. The main difference is that MPR gives us a better picture of the long-term results of our actions. Sometimes, we need a **bird' eye view** of the whole process to understand what's working and what's not. That's the whole point of MPR.

The process is quite similar to weekly reviews. Focus on four main areas:

#1 – Performance of the last month: How was your performance in the last four weeks? Why were some weeks more productive than others? Check all parameters. What worked consistently in the last four weeks, and what didn't work out? Identify any roadblocks you came across.

#2 - Current status: Measure your entire last month's progress against the end result(s)? Are you satisfied with the growth rate? Any pending obligations?

#3 - Think outside the box: Are there any missed opportunities? Can you identify any patterns? What can you do to increase your productivity? Brainstorm new ideas.

#4 - Future course of action: What would you do in the next thirty days? Do you keep going like this or do you need to make adjustments? Plan your next four weeks.

The MPR helps you take in the bigger picture of the progress that you are making. It helps you identify any hidden patterns, missed opportunities, persistent problems, and high-priority activities. Once you start doing MPR, the whole process becomes transparent, resulting in a noticeable boost in productivity.

> *"I think it's very important to have a feedback loop, where you're constantly thinking about what you have done and how you could be doing it better."* – **Elon Musk**, business magnate, designer, engineer, and CEO.

Summary

- Conducting monthly performance reviews (MPR) is useful for getting a **bird' eye view** of the whole process.

- The main difference between weekly performance reviews and MPR is that the latter gives us a better picture of the long-term results of our actions.

- Again, use the 4-step process to identify any hidden patterns, missed opportunities, persistent problems, and high-priority activities over a period of a month.

- The MPR helps you take in the bigger picture of the progress that you are making, helping the whole process become transparent and streamlined.

57. The Universal Performance Disruptor At Workplace

The Problem

A clutter-filled workspace increases the opportunities for distraction. Whether it's an array of electronic devices or just a piling mound of work creating a big mess on your desk, these things should be properly put in their place.

While a few scattered piles of paper might seem harmless enough, a research project, conducted by Stephanie McMains and Sabine Kastner, suggest that clutter can have a negative impact on our attention and focus.

Link to the published article:
https://pubmed.ncbi.nlm.nih.gov/21228167/

Our brains prefer organized workspaces. Being exposed to clutter makes it harder for us to focus our attention.

Another research paper, co-authored by John M. Gaspar and his peers, point out the fact that the presence of visual clutter has a detrimental impact on the brain's working memory.

Link to the paper:
https://www.pnas.org/content/early/2016/02/17/1523471113

Organize your workspace and reduce the clutter to a bare minimum. You'll notice it's much easier to work productively when your workspace is clean and organized.

The Procrastination Solution

One of the best techniques for overcoming procrastination is to get everything in order before you sit down and start working.

When your workspace is neat & clean, and everything is in place, it has a positive effect on your mind. You'll *want* to get started and keep working.

My office gives me a huge boost of energy because I meditate and drink green tea as soon as I get to my office. My office is quite well organized. I have arranged everything to my taste. I have lights according to my liking. I have a specific smell in my office that I really like. You want everything about your workspace to make you feel good.

I have seen offices of a lot of entrepreneurs where everything looks messed up. Very cluttered and disorganized. All the other rooms are nice & tidy but their office looks like a warzone. It's rough. There is trash all around. It just looks messy. You want your workplace to look pleasant. You want to trigger pleasant emotions as you enter your office.

The most productive people arrange their workspace so the workspace looks good and feels comfortable. A neat and clean workspace puts you in the right mindset to take action.

Here Are Some Guidelines to Declutter Your Workspace:

#1 - Start by clearing your work desk so that there's no clutter. Put everything on the shelves. Throw all unnecessary things in the dustbin. Make it look clean.

#2 – Now, collect the things that you need to finish the task. Put them on your desk so they are right in front of you.

#3 – Arrange your workspace so it's comfortable because you'll be spending a long period of time here. Give special attention to your chair. Make sure it provides good back and thigh support. Use a cushion if you need to. The height of your desk should not be too high or low. You should not feel any strain in your body while doing work.

Whenever you aren't sure about keeping something or not, ask yourself, *"what is the purpose of it?"* You'll find that many things have fulfilled their purpose and now can be stored or thrown out.

Cleaning up your office once or twice will not be enough. You'll find that clutter always starts to build up again. Set five minutes each day or an hour a week to clean your workspace. Make it a routine.

Many studies have already proven the psychological benefits of decluttering your home and office. Take the time to declutter your workspace and start noticing the positive changes that occur.

It's a tiny commitment that will pay off forever.

> *"For every minute spent organizing, an hour is earned."* – **Benjamin Franklin**, one of the founding fathers of the United States.

Summary

- Clutter increases the opportunities for distraction which could lead to procrastination.

- Research shows that clutter can have a negative impact on our attention, focus, and working memory.

- Organize your workspace and reduce it to the bare minimum. You'll notice it's much easier to work productively when your setting is clean and organized.

- Use the above guidelines to declutter your workspace for better productivity.

58. The Quiet Time: Why, When, And How

The Problem

During the day, there are lots of things which demand our attention like work, family responsibilities, hobbies, friends, etc. When caught up in our daily grind, we get distracted and lose track of our own agenda.

For instance, maybe your friends start calling you to hang out. Or you suddenly receive an email demanding an urgent response. You can even get distracted by irrelevant messages that pop up on your phone.

You also have some obligations like your day job or picking the kids from school. These are non-negotiable in nature and can consume a lot of your attention.

No wonder it's hard to maintain focus.

The Procrastination Solution

If your days are too chaotic to maintain focus and get work done, try to schedule your most important tasks in the early morning. I realize many people are not accustomed to early mornings, but there are a lot of benefits of working before sunrise.

The first and most obvious benefit is that the environment is quieter. There are no noises. Phones are not ringing. Kids are not crying. There are no neighbors shouting or playing loud music.

The environment is quiet and calm. Usually, there is a wonderful pin-drop silence. Make the most of it. Get up before the world wakes up and get your most important tasks (MIT) done without any outside interferences.

Here's the second benefit. In the early morning, you are free from all urgent demands that pop up later during the day. There are no emails that require an immediate response. There are no calls from work. Your friends don't call you at five o'clock in the morning to make plans for Saturday evening. You don't get bombarded with constant notifications on your phone screaming for your attention. Your mind is free from all the requests that the world places upon you later in the day. Make use of this distraction-free time.

The third benefit of working in the morning is that there are no obligations this early in the day. You don't have to go to work at this time, nor you have to mow the lawn or drop kids off at school. Everyone is sleeping. There is only you and this quiet moment. And you have it all for yourself. You can use it however you want.

Let's recap the benefits of working early: Your mind is fresh. The environment is calm. You don't get disturbed. You have no obligations. This makes early mornings the most productive time of the day, especially if your daytime is quite demanding.

If you often find yourself distracted during the day, the morning time is a boon for you. It might be the only time you have to work on your goals undisturbed. Make full use of it.

Your day is usually dictated by how you spend your first hour. If you win the morning, you win the day.

> "There is no magic formula to success. I wake up early in the morning, generally around 4 o'clock, and do my cardio on an empty stomach. Stretch, have a big breakfast, and then I'll go train."

— **Dwayne "The Rock" Johnson**, Hollywood actor, producer, and winner of ten world heavyweight championships in professional wrestling.

Summary

- Sometimes, our hectic schedule during the daytime takes a toll on our productivity.

- If your days are too chaotic, try to schedule your most important tasks early in the morning.

- The environment is quieter. There are no distractions. There are no obligations. It makes early mornings the most productive time of the day.

- Let the first hour of the day set the tone of success and productivity that gets carried throughout the day.

59. The Contribution Of Personal Analytics

The Problem

Another common cause of distraction is information overload. We consume a huge amount of information in just one day and become so overwhelmed that we end up not taking action at all. Some call it "paralysis by analysis." We tend to gather so much data, so much information that now we are confused about how to apply all that information.

When you have *one problem* and *one solution*, it's easy to take action. But when you have one problem and a *hundred solutions*, it confuses the heck out of us. Now we become too hesitant to try anything. It almost always leads to procrastination.

The procrastination Solution

The key is to stop consuming information passively and start engaging with the ideas we learn. A great tool for that is – Reflective writing. In other words, writing in a journal at night to reflect on the day.

It turns out that journaling can be used to train our focus and strengthen neural pathways. A research document published by Stacy E. Walker from Ball State University suggests that journaling can help you by enhancing reflection, critical thinking, and decision making.

Link to research:
https://www.ncbi.nlm.nih.gov/pmc/articles/PMC1472640/

Journaling is a proven method to gain more clarity and make better decisions (i.e., choosing to act now rather than later). Let's look at how to start journaling and get the benefits.

How to Start Journaling?

The key here is to make it as easy & accessible as possible, so you don't miss it. Here are some tips that help you get started:

1. **Night time is the best.** To get the most benefits of reflective journaling, try to do it at night before sleep. This will allow you to analyze everything that happened during the day.

2. **Use a pen and paper.** Using the old-fashioned pen and paper for journaling is one of the most important tips that I can give you. Studies have proven that using pen and paper for journaling provides amazing psychological and productivity benefits. Writing by hand is superior to typing on a computer or mobile phone. It improves memory, encourages deeper thinking and reflection, and builds new neural connections in the brain.

Link to study:
https://journals.sagepub.com/doi/abs/10.1177/0956797614524581

3. **Write only a few bullet points.** You don't have to write full sentences. A few bullet points for interesting or important things that happened each day are sufficient. I usually write 2-3, though sometimes I write 5-6 if a lot of things have happened. I put personal and work stuff together. By keeping things short and simple, it's easy to finish the day's entry in a few minutes!

However, if you would like to go into more details and spend more time journaling, that's even better as it fleshes things out even more.

4. **Keep your notebook where you won't miss it.** I put my notebook right beside my bed. When I see the notebook as I sit down on my bed, I pick it up and start journaling. This ensures that I never forget to journal at night.

That's it. Reflective journaling works very well for my clients and me. It allows us to analyze the events that happened, reflect on what we learned, and chart a new course of action – all leading to improved productivity at work.

> *"Without reflection, we go blindly on our way, creating more unintended consequences, and failing to achieve anything useful."* – **Margaret J. Wheatley**, American writer and management consultant.

Summary

- A common cause of procrastination is information overload. We tend to consume a huge amount of information, become overwhelmed, and end up not taking action at all.

- The answer is to stop consuming information passively and start engaging with the ideas we learn.

- Studies have proven that journaling can enhance reflection, critical thinking, and decision-making by analyzing what we learned during the day.

- Use the tips provided above to start reflective journaling. This simple activity has the potential to completely transform your work life.

60. Harmonize Scattered Bonds

The Problem

Sometimes we procrastinate because we are unable to focus on the task at hand. While there could be a number of reasons behind our lack of focus, we are going to discuss something that often doesn't get talked about.

Effect of Relationships on Productivity

There are hidden aspects that rob you of focus. Sometimes in life, we have some unresolved relationship issues - that may not be apparent on the surface - affecting everything in our lives. They touch every part of our existence and influence what we say, do, and think.

If you are unable to focus on work, or feel exhausted, or experience a lack of motivation, the reason behind it could be as simple as having a bad relationship with one of your family members, friends, or co-workers.

It causes a lot of inner stress. Maybe you had a fight six months ago and didn't talk to them since. It was not properly resolved. You might not think about that consciously, but your subconscious mind doesn't forget, and it takes a toll on your ability to focus and feel motivated.

These issues need to be sorted out and resolved. If not, then it will be like a hole in the bucket that drains out your focus. It will always be operating at the back of your mind, sucking out your energy.

Proper closure is needed. And fortunately, that is possible in almost all cases.

Here's what I would do to sort out any unresolved relationship issues:

1. If it is possible to call them:

- Get yourself in a calm mood and call them.

- Calmly tell them something along the lines of "what happened in the past is now over, and I am ready to move on. Please let it all go and move on."

- Be a bigger person and forgive them if they wronged you in the past. Or ask for forgiveness if it was your fault.

- Wish them well for the future and end the call.

- Whether they respond positively or negatively, it's fine either way. What's important is that you took steps to resolve the issue from your side. You will feel calmer like a burden was removed from your shoulders.

2. If it is not possible to call them:

Sometimes, you cannot call the person due to many reasons (they might not be alive, or you can't make yourself call them, or you don't have their contact, etc.). Don't worry. There is still a way to resolve the issue even without contacting the other person.

Letter of Forgiveness Technique

A very effective way to let go of the intense emotions trapped inside is to write down all of your thoughts on a blank piece of paper. This is your *letter of forgiveness*. You can let out everything that you wanted to say to the people who wronged you in the past (or ask for forgiveness if you made a mistake).

Go all out. Write down all the things you want to say to them and how you really feel inside. Keep expressing until you empty your mind and emotions.

Now you do not have to send this letter. You can go ahead and throw it away after you wrote all that you wanted to say.

Now it cannot be virtual paper (on a computer or smartphone). This exercise is a lot more effective when done on physical paper with a pen. Writing your thoughts down on a piece of paper has a much more profound impact on our minds.

One of the reasons we feel stressed when thinking of bad memories is because there are a lot of unexpressed/suppressed emotions we have inside. As long as we keep holding our thoughts and emotions inside and don't express them, they will turn toxic. Over time, pent-up emotions tend to get stronger in their intensity which can be very detrimental to our mental and emotional well-being.

To let go of the past, write down everything you want to say. Fully express yourself. Nobody is going to see this letter except you anyway, so go all out. Eventually, you will reach a point where you start feeling calmer. This is the place where we wanted to arrive at.

With the newfound calmer mind, write how you would harm your present and future if you keep holding on to the past and write down - *"Even though I don't agree with what you did... I forgive you anyway."*

Again, don't type it on the computer or phone. Write it down on paper. You will immediately start feeling better. You are letting out suppressed emotions and thoughts. After you are finished with all of it, you can throw it away if you want.

Your emotions and rage when you think about the past will be reduced. And if you repeat this exercise for 10-14 days, you will create a drastic change in how you feel about your past.

> *"Inner peace begins the moment you choose not to allow another person or event to control your emotions."* – **Pema Chodron**, American Tibetan Buddhist, teacher, and author.

Summary:

- If you are unable to focus on work, or feel exhausted, or experience a lack of motivation, the reason behind it could be an unresolved relationship issue with one of your family members, friends, or co-workers.

- These issues need to be sorted out and resolved. And fortunately, that is possible in most cases.

- If it's possible to contact the other person, use the tips provided to peacefully resolve the issue.

- If you cannot contact them for any reason, use the *letter of forgiveness* technique.

- It takes a lot of courage but the peace of mind, along with the boost in productivity that ensues, is worth the effort.

Section V
How To Get More Done in Less Time

Sometimes, you might be looking to get more done in less time. This situation is quite frequent and can be caused by a number of reasons. For instance, your manager gave you a project with a very short deadline. Or you procrastinated on filing your taxes, and the last date is approaching. Or you didn't get to study because of travel, and now the exams are just around the corner.

You will face many situations in which you would be looking to get more done in a short period of time. It can be difficult because of work overload. You'll find that there's too much to do. As soon as you finish with one task, another pops up. And you seem never to catch up.

In this section, we will discuss strategies that will help you meet very short deadlines. Once you master these techniques, getting more done in a short period of time won't be a problem.

61. The "Now" Element

The Problem

If you are looking to get more done in a short time-period, then one of the challenges you'll come across is tackling multiple objectives at once.

Studies have proven that multitasking can reduce your productivity by a significant amount.

A study conducted by David Mayer (Ph.D.) in 2001 suggested that multitasking can reduce your productivity by up to 40 percent! The reason behind it is that our mind takes some time to adjust when we shift from one activity to another. Therefore, the back and forwards between multiple tasks can lead to a considerable amount of wasted time.

In reality, multitasking does the opposite of what we think it does. Instead of accomplishing many things at once, it slows down the progress in each of your objectives. We end up wasting more time and effort.

There are better options for being productive than juggling too many things at once.

The Procrastination Solution

What is the best way to get more things done in less time?

Only focus on the **'now element'** at any given moment.

Your 'now element' is the ONE task that is the most important AND most urgent at this moment.

It has to be both - **important** and **urgent**. It has to be done and done quickly.

If a task is important but not urgent, schedule it for later. If a task is urgent but not important, delegate it to someone else. Right now, you should only focus on a task that is important AND urgent, i.e., your '**now element**'.

Note about "urgent and important" – this concept is derived from Eisenhower's Matrix and is explained in chapter 68 in greater detail.

Focus on it with your complete attention until it gets done. Do not focus on anything else.

All successful people know the importance of focusing on a single task for a period of time. Napoleon Hill, the author of the famed *Think and Grow Rich,* advocates that intensely focusing on a single objective is the starting point for achieving all success, money, and happiness you desire.

This single idea has changed millions of people's lives and will continue to transform even more lives in the future. It's time for you to embrace this concept as well.

> *"It is those who concentrate on but one thing at a time advance in this world."* – **Og Mandino**, Author of the bestseller *The Greatest Salesman in the World.*

Summary

- Multi-tasking can reduce your productivity by up to 40%!

- Your best option is to focus on ONE task, which is the most important AND most urgent at this moment.

- Focus on it with your complete attention until it gets done. After it's finished, move on to the next one.

- Working in this efficient manner will maximize your probability of getting more done in less time.

62. Prerequisite Of Unparalleled Performance

The Problem

Sometimes, you are not able to work efficiently because your mind is not calm. You are struggling and overwhelmed with negative thoughts. For instance, you might be worried about your job, debt repayment, problems with your relationships, or even something related to health. There can be any number of reasons behind your worry.

A troubled mind is not interested in being productive. When you are worried or angry or depressed, it's tough to work efficiently. We need a calm state of mind. You will be able to concentrate on work and be productive only when your mind is quiet.

While some workplace stress is normal, excessive stress can hinder your productivity & performance, impact your physical and emotional health, and affect your home or office relationships.

Whatever your ambition or work demands, there are steps you can take to protect yourself from the damaging effects of stress, improving your job satisfaction, and bolstering your well-being in and out of the workplace.

The Procrastination Solution

We must learn to quieten our minds.

An effective way to do this is exercise. Obviously, there are physical benefits to exercise, but it can also do wonders for your mind. Any exercise that challenges you to keep moving is a great distraction from what's going on in your head. Physical activities like cardio, strength training, yoga, walking, kickboxing, and dancing - all force you to focus in different ways.

Exercise puts you in a good mood due to the increased secretion of 'feel-good' chemicals in the body like endorphin, dopamine, and serotonin. Additionally, the increased core temperature of the body leads to relaxed muscles, which lower anxiety and stress levels. Deep breathing during exercise makes your mind calm and relaxed. You become more focused and energized. Exercise stimulates the growth of neurons in the parts of the brain which are damaged by stress and depression.

A Study in 2010 found that three sessions of yoga per week resulted in increased secretion of GABA, a hormone related to improving mood and lifting depression. Results established exercise as one of the best things you can do to protect yourself from anxiety and depression.

Another way to way to achieve a quiet mind is through meditation. You knew this one was coming, right? Meditation is so important for anyone who spends most of their time thinking and worrying because it encourages you to be still without reacting to your thoughts. There are numerous studies that confirm the profound benefits of meditation on the mind. Refer to chapter 89 in the last section of the book.

If you have never done meditation before, I have some good news - practicing meditation is very simple, and you won't have to dwell on any religious aspects that people associate with meditation.

At its core, meditation is simply a practice of focusing on your breath. That's it. None of the religious associations is necessary if you are an atheist. For an easy step-by-step guide to meditation, check out chapter 89.

Just follow the simple instructions and start doing meditation daily. You will be pleasantly surprised by the effect on your emotional state. You will be a lot more relaxed and focused.

Exercising and meditating regularly will be enough for the majority of people to achieve a calmer state of mind. But in some cases, people might still need something more to deal with stress and worry. These people will find the last section of this book incredibly important and valuable.

It contains several effective exercises to get rid of negative emotions and thoughts. It is dedicated to getting into a calmer and productive state of mind. Refer to it when needed.

"The mind is like water. When it is turbulent, it's difficult to see. When it is calm, everything becomes clear." – **Buddhism.**

Summary

• A troubled mind is not productive. When you are worried or angry or depressed, it's difficult to get yourself focusing on doing any work.

• You will be able to concentrate on your work and be productive only when your mind is quiet.

• Exercise puts you in a good mood due to the increased secretion of 'feel-good' chemicals in the body like endorphin, dopamine, and serotonin. The increased core temperature of the body leads to relaxed muscles, which lower anxiety and stress levels.

• Another way to achieve a quiet mind is through meditation. It is important for anyone who spends most of their time thinking and worrying because it encourages you to be still and quiet without reacting to your thoughts.

63. The Game Of Divide And Conquer

The Problem

Sometimes, we get overwhelmed by seeing the amount of work we have to do in a short amount of time. Or we find a task so boring that we can't make ourselves do it. It reduces our motivation, and we start procrastinating.

Here's an amazing technique to get more done throughout the day.

The Procrastination Solution

Divide your workday into small blocks of high performance.

The main idea behind this technique is that any large task can be broken down into short-timed intervals called "blocks." Each interval is followed by a short break.

For instance, if you work for eight hours a day, divide it into eight blocks of one-hour periods. Each of the one-hour periods will be followed by a small break to refresh the mind and body.

This technique is particularly helpful when you can't motivate yourself to do a task because it's either too overwhelming or incredibly dull.

According to research done on the importance of short breaks between tasks, it was found that:

1. Planned breaks can vastly improve focus.

Link to study:
https://www.sciencedaily.com/releases/2011/02/110208131529.htm

2. Breaks allow the brain to process new information.

Link to study:
https://journals.sagepub.com/doi/abs/10.1177/1745691612447308

The effectiveness of dividing work into short segments cannot be understated. It has been *proven* to bring measurable improvements in productivity.

To get started, tell yourself that you'll only do one small block. Since one block is a small commitment, it's easier to get started. When you finish the first one, you wouldn't want to stop because you have built momentum. At this point, it's easy to keep working until the work is finished.

Here's the step-by-step process:

Pre-requisite: Get an alarm. You can use the alarm on your mobile phone or computer if you wish. I prefer the alarm on my mobile phone.

Step 1 – Choose a task that needs to be done.
Step 2 – Set the alarm to 60 minutes.
Step 3 – Work on the task until the alarm goes off.
Step 4 – Take a break for 5-10 minutes. Get up and move around during this time. Do not stay at the spot you were working. You can take a short walk, grab a coffee, do stretching, meditate, listen to a song, or any relaxing activity. The main point of the break is to get your mind off work and relax.

Return to your tasks and repeat until the work is finished.

Here are a few helpful tips. During your one-hour work periods, make sure that there are no distractions. The uninterrupted focus for the 60-minute duration is the whole point here. Put your mobile phone on silent mode. Don't answer emails, check social media, or do anything else. Focus only on the work at hand. Answer all phone calls and email requests after the work hour is complete.

What About the Duration?

Some people ask if the duration of these work periods can be changed. Yes. Everyone is different. For some people, one-hour blocks may be too small, and for others, one hour may be too much.

These blocks can range from 15 minutes to 90 minutes. But do not go more than 90 minutes without taking a break because then you're really pushing it. After that point, the quality of your work starts diminishing.

I always use this technique whenever I am working on a difficult project. I, personally, like to work for 30 minutes and take a 5-minute break to refresh my mind. Some people I work with prefer 20 minutes. Some prefer 45 minutes. Everyone is different. You need to test different timings to find the one that suits you the best.

You should definitely try this technique. When implemented properly, it's one of the best tools to beat procrastination and increase productivity.

> "All great things are done by a series of small things brought together." – **Vincent Van Gogh**. One of the most influential figures in the history of western art.

Summary

- It's common to procrastinate when your work is either too overwhelming or incredibly boring.

- A great way to handle such tasks is to divide your workday into small blocks of high performance.

● Since one block is a small commitment, it's easier to get started. When you finish the first one, you won't want to stop because you have built momentum.

● Use the guidelines above to implement this technique. It's one of the best for getting more done in less time.

64. Cycle Of Mental Rejuvenation

The Problem

For many people, burnout is a huge roadblock to getting more done in less time. The mental and physical exhaustion makes it seem like an impossible task.

It's pretty common in today's demanding work culture. But some highly productive people seemed to found a way to avoid getting burned out. For instance, what about pro-athletes? They need to push past their physical and mental limits and perform at the highest level possible. They must be having frequent burnouts, right?

Not really.

All high-performing individuals, whether in business or sports, know a secret to high performance. That secret allows them to operate at peak levels of performance for extended periods of time.

What's the secret?

Optimizing the recovery time.

The Procrastination Cure

Taking breaks to recover physically and mentally is one of the most vital yet overlooked aspects of our work culture. In sports, all athletes and coaches know the importance of recovery. Without proper rest, it's almost impossible to perform at the highest capacity.

Here are a few benefits of taking a break as proven by studies:

1. Taking shorts breaks creates higher work engagement in employees.

Link:
https://psycnet.apa.org/record/2018-12793-001

2. Even very short breaks improve attention levels.

Link:
https://www.sciencedirect.com/science/article/abs/pii/S0272494415000328

3. Taking frequent breaks leads to increased creativity and problem-solving skills.

Link:
https://onlinelibrary.wiley.com/doi/abs/10.1002/jocb.88

These are only a few examples of how beneficial breaks are. There are many other benefits. The point is that we should start looking at the break in a different light. Breaks are never a waste of time. The right kind of break has the potential to double your productivity and results.

Take breaks throughout the day to refresh your mind and body. If you follow the previous section of one-hour work sessions followed by a 10-minute break, make sure that break rejuvenates you. While you can do whatever you wish during that time, it's better to optimize your break to help you become more productive in the next work session.

How to Optimize Your Breaks?

Not all breaks are equally effective. For instance, if a person spends their breaks eating fast food or smoking cigarettes, then the whole point of a break is lost. We have to ensure that our breaks recover and rejuvenate us.

Here are some excellent options for breaks:

1. Walk for a few minutes. Physical movements increase blood flow, which boosts brain function, restoring your energy, focus, and creativity.

2. Stretch. Stretching relaxes the muscles, lowers stress, and refreshes the mind.

3. Meditate for a few minutes. Meditation calms the mind and provides deep relaxation.

4. Watch something funny. Laughter is the best medicine. It releases stress, fills you up with positive emotions, and energizes the mind.

5. Listen to your favorite music. The power of music never ceases to amaze. Listening to your favorite music during the breaks is one of the best ways to rejuvenate the mind.

6. Deep breathing. Taking some deep breaths for a few minutes helps you calm down and get centered. It's a powerful way to get back in control.

7. Talk to your friends. A classic way of refreshing your mood. Try each one of these.

When you try different kinds of breaks, you will find that some breaks work better for you than others. Be mindful of the results and stick to the ones that work best for you.

Breaks are equally as important as taking action. A narrow focus on action while ignoring recovery will almost certainly lead to exhaustion and burnout. Research studies have already confirmed the profound benefits of rest and recovery on our focus, attention span, energy, and productivity.

Never be afraid to take time out to rest and recover. Even 30-minutes of proper rest can result in several hours of increased productivity and performance.

"Rest is extremely important to me. I need to rest and recover in order for the training I do to be absorbed by my body." – **Usain Bolt**, Jamaican eight-time Olympic gold medalist, widely considered to be the greatest sprinter of all time.

Summary

- Breaks are equally as important as taking action.

- Optimizing your rest and recovery is needed to perform at the highest efficiency.

- Try experimenting with the different kinds of breaks to find what suits you the best.

65. The "Hardest-First" Technique

The Problem

When you are looking to get things done quickly, a common obstacle you will face is work overload. There is too much to do. As soon as you finish with one thing, another pops up. And you never seem to catch up.

The way to get out of this predicament is to identify your most important tasks and get them done first. Once the critical tasks are out of the way, you can focus on the remaining work. Finishing your most important task (MIT) for the day will significantly impact your results.

Just this single concept has the potential to double your productivity.

The Procrastination Solution

Here's what needs to be done: When you start your workday, look at your to-do list. Usually, you will find one task that is the most difficult to do but has the biggest impact on your results. It is usually the task that you procrastinate on the most often.

You should start your day by working on your most difficult task and get it done as soon as possible. Do your best to ignore all distractions like checking your emails, etc. Discipline yourself to get started on your most demanding work first.

After it's finished, you'll have the satisfaction of knowing that the worst part of your work is over. Everything will be easier from this point. Another reason is that you have the most mental bandwidth and energy at the start of the day. As the day goes on, you naturally become more and more tired.

The most difficult task should be handled when you are in the most energetic and resourceful state, i.e., at the start of the day.

Few Things to Note:

1. If you have more than one priority task, start with the most difficult one. Once it's done, move on to the next one.

2. The more you delay working on the MIT, the worse the situation will become. As a rule of thumb, once you have identified what needs to be done, get started as quickly as possible. The more you delay, the harder it will be to get started.

Once you get into the habit of finishing your MIT the first thing in the morning, your workday would feel completely transformed. It releases a lot of stress from your job and sets the tone for the whole day. When you begin on a high note, you build momentum. You start strong and finish strong.

> "***Every morning is a fresh start***" – T.S. Eliot, One of the 20th century's most influential poets.

Summary

- Overburdened with work is one of the most prominent causes of procrastination.

- To resolve this problem, identify your most difficult task(s) for the day.

- Start your workday by working on your most challenging and difficult task and get it done as soon as possible.

- When you start strong, you build momentum that carries throughout the day.

66. Implementation Of Parkinson's Law

The Problem

Often, we procrastinate because we think there's too much time left to complete the task. We tell ourselves, *"I'll do it later. There is no hurry"*. Not only does it make us waste precious time, but it also creates a lot of stress in our minds. No matter how much we try to divert our minds by watching TV, playing games, hanging out in the bar, or going surfing, our unfinished task is always in the back of our minds.

"I still have to complete that work."

It robs us of any peace of mind. We are continuously stressed until we finally buckle down and work on the task.

The Procrastination Solution

Here's an excellent solution to the *"there's too much time left. I'll do it later"* syndrome:

Use Parkinson's Law in your favor.

I use Parkinson's Law on a regular basis, and it increased my productivity by quite a bit, and it can do so for you as well.

What Is Parkinson's Law?

Parkinson's Law is based on an article written by British historian and author Cyril Northcote Parkinson for The Economist in 1955. It was later referred in a book titled *Parkinson's Law: The Pursuit of Progress*.

Parkinson's Law asserts that *"work expands to fill the time available for its completion."* For instance, if you have a two-hour task but give yourself two days to complete it, the task will (psychologically) become more complex to fill out the two-day time limit. You will deal with a lot more issues and face unexpected challenges. As a result, you'll barely be able to finish the task in two days. A lot of the extra time is spent procrastinating and stressing over how to get it done.

The opposite is also true. If you usually take 10-days to finish a task but set out to complete it in 5-days, you will find a way to do that. For instance, have you seen an employee who starts working on the weekly report a day before the due date and successfully manages to pull it off? Or a student who starts studying three days before the exams but ends up getting good grades. That is Parkinson's Law in essence.

It can be used in a more refined way, so that you will not have to pull all-nighters at the very last minute. You'll be able to finish the task before the deadline effortlessly.

What Does Science Say?

Parkinson's Law is quite well documented in time management literature. An article published by researchers Judith F. Bryan and Edwin A. Locke supported the validity of Parkinson's Law. In a study, two groups were told to complete a task. The only difference was in the time allotted to finish it. Group 1 was given twice as much time needed to do it. Group 2 was assigned just enough time to finish it.

After three rounds, it was found that group 1 utilized the extra time they had to finish the task. They were slow to complete the task. On the other hand, group 2 finished the same task within the smaller time frame they were allotted. Both results were in accordance with Parkinson's Law.

Link to the research article:
https://www.sciencedirect.com/science/article/abs/pii/0030507367900219

How to Apply Parkinson's Law?

Start by setting the deadline to half of what was set before. If you had to finish a work in 10 days, reduce the deadline to 5 days. For example, if today is Monday and your boss asks you to submit a sales report by next Monday, you'll finish it by Thursday.

It creates an urgency to finish the work. You end up eliminating all distractions and become laser-focused on getting the job done.

Parkinson's Law Can Be Applied in Three Steps:

Step #1 – Examine the work that needs to be done.

Step #2 – Estimate how much time you'll need to finish it realistically. That's your normal deadline.

Step #3 – Reduce your normal deadline by 50%. That's your new timeframe to get the task done.

Start the work.

Research has shown that a reduction in the deadline leads to big boosts in productivity without sacrificing work quality.

Things to Note:

If you could not finish the task within the new deadline, you need to examine your work sessions. What stopped you from meeting the deadline? And what can you do to eliminate these obstacles?

• Are you constantly distracted by emails or other people? Maybe you need to shift your work sessions to a quieter time like early morning.

• Are you busy with many other obligations? See if you could delegate some non-critical work to other people.

The point here is to find out if there are any obstacles in your path. Is anything stopping you from working with 100% focus?

If you are working with 100% focus and still not able to reach the deadline, then maybe you need to adjust the deadline. Maybe you should reduce the deadline to 60% instead of 50%. Maybe that's your sweet spot. The only way to find your sweet spot is by experimentation. Try different deadlines (50% - 60% - 65% -70%) and determine which one suits you the best.

Even if you find your preferred deadline to be 70%, you're still saving 30% of your time by applying Parkinson's Law. That's an incredible achievement by any standard.

> "A person who dares to waste one hour of time has not discovered the value of life." – **Charles Darwin**, English geologist and biologist, and the founder of evolution theory.

Summary

• Often, we procrastinate because we have too much time left to complete the task.

• Use the Parkinson's Law to get rid of "There's still time. I'll do it later" syndrome.

• Parkinson's Law asserts that *"work expands to fill the time available for its completion."*

- Estimate how much time you'll need to realistically finish a task. And reduce it to 50%-60%. That's your new timeframe to get the job done.

- Research has shown that a reduction in the deadline leads to a significant boost in productivity without sacrificing the work quality.

67. Fabrication Of Mental Road-Map

The Problem

There are two types of mornings we all have: Some days we wake up feeling on top of the world, and other days we wish we could go back to sleep. Mornings can make or break the whole day. If we get up and launch ourselves into those tasks & obligations straight away, we lose control of our day.

For example, if the first thing you do is to check emails as soon as you wake up, you are in reaction to the world. Instead of planning what you need to accomplish today, you get caught up in other people's agendas and spend the whole day managing their demands.

The Procrastination Solution

To take charge of the day, you need to gain control over your mornings. A morning visualization practice is a great way to do just that. It provides stability & direction to your day. You'll no longer get caught in the web of other people's demands and requests. You'll decide what is to be done and when it'll be done, and how it'll be done. You'll have full control over your day.

Morning visualization is a very effective way to gain direction and increase motivation. A study conducted by researchers J. E. Driskell, C. Copper, and A. Moran concluded that mental practice/visualization could have a significant positive impact on performance.

Link to study:
https://psycnet.apa.org/doiLanding?doi=10.1037%2F0021-9010.79.4.481

Regular practice of morning visualization exposes your mind to your goals vividly. This detailed exposure makes your subconscious mind accept your goals as your target and makes your RAS (reticular activating system) focus on achieving them.

You'll feel an increased 'urge' to go for your goals. It's not a logical thought. It's a feeling. And feelings are the primary drivers of human behavior. When your emotions are on your side, it becomes natural to take action.

On the other hand, logical thinking is ineffective when your emotions are opposing you. For example, suppose you have to do your taxes, but you are relaxing and watching the TV. Your mind is at rest, and you aren't in a mood to do anything. It will be a LOT HARDER to logically convince yourself that you should turn off the TV and open your tax file.

It can be done, but the chances of logic overcoming emotions are very slim.

This is where morning visualization comes into the picture. It aligns your emotions with your goals, so there is no friction between the two. How easy do you think it will be when your thoughts and feelings are on the same side? Going with the tax example, your thoughts would be telling you to do your taxes, and you feel an emotional compulsion to do it as well.

Now, what are your chances to turn off the TV and do your taxes?

Morning visualization is so effective that it sometimes feels like magic. Whether you believe in the law of attraction (as in 'the secret') or not, sometimes it seems as if visualization has more power than we understand.

Much research has been done on visualization in recent times and its positive effects have been widely accepted by researchers worldwide.

According to a research paper published by Stewart L. Ross on the effectiveness of visualization in improving trombone performance, the addition of visualization or mental practice to the trombone training was found to be very beneficial.

Link to study:
https://journals.sagepub.com/doi/abs/10.2307/3345249

Visualization is widely used by top athletes, entrepreneurs, success coaches, celebrities, and other people who are at the top in their respective fields.

• Jim Carrey used visualization to achieve stardom and become a multi-millionaire in 5 years.

• Arnold Schwarzenegger had pictures and a poster of Reg Park, his idol. He constantly imagined his body shaping up like Reg's. In his own words, "the more I focused in on this image and worked, the more I saw it was real and possible for me to be like him." He went on to become the most awarded bodybuilder of his time.

• Tiger Woods, the ultra-successful golfer, was taught to visualize by his father in his childhood, and he has used it ever since. During his matches, he visualizes the ball going exactly where he wants it to go and then makes a shot. He became one of the most successful and wealthiest golfers in history.

• Will Smith, the famous Hollywood actor, gives a lot of credit for his success to visualization. In his mind, he always imagined himself as being an A-list Hollywood celebrity. He said "in my mind, I was always a Hollywood superstar. You all just don't know it yet."

There are countless examples of successful people who used visualization to boost their motivation and conviction for their objectives. I can personally vouch for the effectiveness of visualization. My first book was pending for more than one year, and somehow, I always found a reason to avoid it.

Frustrated at my behavior, I started visualizing regularly that my book is finished within six months. Soon I started experiencing increased motivation to sit down and write. What's more, I started neglecting the previous excuses that used to stop me from writing. As a result, I completed that book in a little over six months.

How to practice morning visualization?

The practice of visualization is quite simple.

1. First, sit or lie down in a relaxed, quiet environment. Make sure there are no distractions like excessive noise or lights. You should feel relaxed in this environment. For most people, such a place would be their bedroom.

2. Close your eyes. Take a few deep, relaxed breaths. Consciously relax your body and mind.

3. Once you are feeling relaxed, start imagining that you have accomplished all tasks on your to-do list. And now that everything is done, you are filled with excitement & joy. Imagine it in as much detail as possible. It should be easy because it's something that you really want. You will start feeling really good.

Note: Don't worry. You don't have to do it perfectly. Just add as many details as you can. After a little practice, you will be able to visualize in much more detail.

4. Now, keep viewing that vision (and feeling good) for a few moments (1 to 5 minutes).

5. Open your eyes and relax.

Wasn't that easy? And it's quite enjoyable too. You feel really good from mentally experiencing your desired goals.
Morning visualization is easy, enjoyable, and VERY POWERFUL. Practice it regularly. In the morning time, the mind is very open to external suggestions. Morning visualization penetrates the mind deeply and brings measurable improvements.

Make the practice of morning visualization a daily habit and reap the rewards forever.

> *"I am a big believer in visualization. I run through my races mentally so that I feel even more prepared."* – **Allyson Felix**, American sprinter and six-time Olympic gold medalist.

Summary

- If you check emails as soon as you wake up, you get caught in other people's agenda and lose control of your day.

- A morning visualization practice is an excellent way to gain control over your mornings.

- Use the visualization exercise to gain clarity of your goals for the day.

- Morning visualization is easy, enjoyable, and effective. It penetrates the mind deeply and brings measurable productivity improvements.

Section VI
What To Do When You Are Overwhelmed With Workload

Sometimes we procrastinate because there are too many things to do. We are not sure how to start. It feels overwhelming. For instance, you arrive at the office and found that you have been delegated additional tasks on top of your already jam-packed schedule. Or maybe you come home and find your entire house messed up by the kids and their friends. Or maybe you moved to a new city and have to arrange everything from scratch.

Being overwhelmed with work is a pretty common ordeal. Responsibilities towards work, home, family, relatives, friends, charity, etc., all pile up and create confusion. We start thinking about how we can manage it. It all seems hopeless.

However, there is much we can do to manage situations like these. In this part, we will look at how to manage an overwhelming workload and get our priority tasks done under any circumstances. If you frequently find yourself spread too thin, then this section will be essential.

68. Identification Of Priorities Using Eisenhower's Matrix

The Problem

You have just received a request to prepare a new report for the next week's presentation. But you already have so many things on your to-do list. Everything looks important... but you don't have enough time to do everything. What would you do?

It's easy to get overwhelmed in these kinds of high-pressure situations. The solution is to prioritize tasks on your to-do list. This critical step will let you know which tasks are important and which ones are distractions.

The Procrastination Solution

Here's another great tool to prioritize tasks in your to-do list: Eisenhower's Matrix.

Dwight D. Eisenhower was a five-star general during World War II and the 34th President of the United States. He invented the Eisenhower principle, which helps in prioritizing tasks by urgency and importance. This concept has been popularized by many publications, most notably "*7 Habits of Highly Effective People*" by Steven Covey.

According to Eisenhower's matrix, all of your tasks can be categorized in four ways:

Category 1 Tasks – Important and Urgent: Some of your tasks are important and need to be done as soon as possible. These should be number one on your priority list. You should personally work on them as soon as possible. Some examples of

"Urgent and Important" tasks could be – Important calls, deadlines, dealing with a problem/crisis, etc.

How to handle category-1 tasks: Do these first. Work on them yourself as soon as possible.

Category 2 Tasks – Important but not Urgent: These tasks don't require your immediate attention but are crucial to your long-term success. Some examples of category-2 tasks are: planning, improving relationship with business partners, improving your customer support, advertising your brand, etc.

How to handle category-2 tasks: Schedule these tasks for later. Come back to them after you finish category 1 tasks.

Category 3 Tasks – Urgent but not Important: You have to get them done, but they don't contribute much to your primary goals. These tasks generally consist of requests made by other people. For example – Your boss asks you to prepare a sales report for last week. You'll have to prepare that report, but it doesn't contribute much to getting your own work done.

How to handle category-3 tasks: Delegate these tasks to other people. These are low-priority activities that stop you from working on your critical tasks. Have other people work on it.

Category 4 Tasks – Not urgent and not Important: These activities don't contribute to your short-term and long-term goals. They are just noise and not necessary at all.

How to handle category-4 tasks: Eliminate these tasks from your to-do list.

Once you start categorizing your tasks, you'll probably find that your priorities are completely changed. You'll notice that you are working on critical tasks more often now. It will result in an immediate increase in your overall productivity level.

"The key is not to prioritize what's on your schedule, but to schedule your priorities." – **Stephen Covey**, American author, businessman, and keynote speaker.

Summary

- It is easy to get overwhelmed when you have too many things on your to-do list.

- Eisenhower's matrix is a great tool to prioritize the tasks you have.

- It helps you to identify what's urgent, what should be delegated, and what should be eliminated.

- Categorizing your work makes it easier to get started, follow-through, and get it done.

69. Utilize The "A.B.C.D.E." Method

The Problem

Oftentimes we procrastinate because there are so many things to do. We are not sure where to begin. It just feels overwhelming.

The Procrastination Solution

The truth is; not all tasks on your to-do list are equally important. Some are more important than others. Some can be delegated. And some should be eliminated without qualms. It's easy to get confused looking at everything on the to-do list.

This is where the ABCDE method can be very helpful. It is a priority-setting system for all of your tasks. It classifies everything into five main groups depending on the order of importance. Due to its effectiveness, the ABCDE method is mentioned quite frequently in productivity literature worldwide.

How to Apply?

The Key to the ABCDE method's effectiveness is its simplicity. It follows a very logical approach and is relatively easy to implement.

Step 1 – Put all your tasks on a list.

Step 2 – Against each task, put A, B, C, D, or E.

Here's what each of them stands for:

• **'A'** stands for the most important tasks. They make the biggest impact on your results. These are critical and should be done first. If you have more than one 'A' task, mark them as A-1, A-2, A-3, and so on.

- **'B'** tasks are valuable but not critically important. These are the task that you *should* do. Finishing 'B' tasks can lead to some benefits, and leaving them unfinished has minor consequences. But these are not as critically important as 'A' tasks. So, as a rule of thumb, never start working on 'B' tasks when you have an 'A' task remaining. Move on to 'B' only when all 'A' tasks are finished.

Some of the examples of 'B' tasks would be checking inbox, replying to emails, preparing slides for next week's presentation, work on the monthly report, and so on.

- **'C'** tasks are your 'nice to do' tasks. They have no direct impact on your goals but have some value for you personally. These tasks could be calling your friends or family, doing a personal favor for your colleague, arranging a farewell party, and so on.

- If a task can be carried out by someone else without downgrading the quality, then that's your **'D'** tasks. These should be delegated to others so you can have more free time to work on your 'A' and 'B' tasks.

- **'E'** stands for the tasks that carry no benefit at all. These are often for personal enjoyment and should be eliminated from your to-do list altogether. Here are some examples of 'E' tasks: Sending funny messages to friends, watching movies, casually spending time on social media, etc.

(Note: It does not mean that hobbies and fun activities have no significance. These are necessary but shouldn't have a place in your 'things-to-accomplish-today' list.)

Step 3 – Carry out the activities in order of importance.

That's it.

This simple technique will revolutionize your work life. You'll be able to declutter your to-do list and identify the priority tasks. Completing these would result in significant improvements in your productivity and results.

"Nobody is too busy. It's just a matter of unresolved priorities." - Unknown

Summary

- Sometimes, we get overwhelmed with the number of tasks on our to-do list.

- This is where the ABCDE method can be very helpful. It is a priority-setting system that classifies everything into five main groups depending on the order of importance.

- Use the guidelines above to prioritize tasks based on the ABCDE method.

- Lastly, carry out the activities in order of importance.

70. The Blueprint For Unflappable Focus

The Problem

Another common cause of procrastination is that sometimes we are not clear about what needs to be done. We have a lot of things running in our minds, but it is all jumbled together. Nothing is outlined in clear and concise words. We lack clarity.

The Procrastination Solution

A great tool for clarity of what we need to do is a daily top-5 checklist. In the morning, make a checklist and put five of your most important tasks in there. No more than that. If you put more than five, it starts to feel like "too much work."

Top-5 checklists are an incredible tool to overcome procrastination and increase productivity daily. When you know what needs to be done today, you have a stronger reason not to give in to the procrastination habit.

Make a list and try to get all of them done each day, but know that it's not always going to happen. On some days, things that aren't directly in your control come up and change your plans. But on average, your productivity levels will go up significantly. You will get a lot more done by adopting this strategy.

Your checklist doesn't have to be perfect. Out of everything you CAN do, choose five things that are most important for today. A great way to find these top five things is to ask yourself these questions:

"Which five activities produce 80% of my results?"

"Which five activities, if completed, would make me feel like I won this day?"

"Which five tasks will make other tasks irrelevant upon completion?"

Here's an example of a top-5 checklist:

1. Workout at the gym in the morning.

2. Meet with the client and pitch our services at 11.00 a.m.

3. Eat a salad with every meal.

4. Spend some time with family in the evening.

5. Read a book for an hour before sleep.

This is an example of a well-balanced checklist, but yours can be vastly different depending on your goals. For someone starting a new business, all 5 of these could be business tasks. The same goes for people trying to lose weight, preparing for their marriage, training for a marathon, and so on. Your checklist is unique and must be tailored to your needs.

Notice that social media, reading news, watching TV, checking email, browsing your favorite sites, sharing photos … none of these are on the list. If you're doing one of these things and not one of your daily checklist items, you're probably not doing the right thing.

Over time, your daily checklist might change. But just having one helps you to evaluate what's essential and what's not.

And when you learn to do this, on an instinctive level, you can begin to let go of procrastination. You can get back to work and smile.

"Effort and courage are not enough without purpose and direction" – **John F. Kennedy**, 35th President of the United States.

Summary

- Procrastination usually occurs when we are not clear about what needs to be done.

- An effective solution is to make a checklist and put five of your most important tasks in there.

- You can find the top most essential tasks of the day by asking the three questions above.

- When you are crystal clear about what needs to be done, you have a stronger reason not to give in to the procrastination habit.

71. The Science Behind 40% Loss In Productivity

The Problem

In our work culture, multitasking is viewed as a good thing. It is considered a sign that the person is busy and productive. However, being busy and being productive are two separate things.

In reality, multitasking creates stress, reduces your creativity, and compromises the quality of your work. When working on an important assignment, multitasking may be your worst enemy.

According to a study conducted by David Mayer, Ph.D., in 2001, multitasking can reduce your productivity by up to 40 percent!

The reason behind it is that our mind takes some time to adjust when we shift from one activity to another. Therefore, the back and forth between multiple tasks can lead to a considerable amount of wasted time.

What's more, when we do several things at once, the quality of our work gets compromised. While multitasking, your mind will be too distracted to develop creative ideas or solve complex problems. Switching back and forth will also make you lose your train of thought, resulting in cutting corners and lowering your work's caliber.

The Procrastination Solution

Here's a better alternative to multitasking: a single-minded focus on one task at any given moment.

Look at your to-do list and select ONE task that needs to be done. Work on it with your complete attention. Do not think about anything else. Once it gets done, move to the next task. Work on it and repeat.

All successful people know the importance of focusing on a single task for a designated time- period. According to Napoleon Hill, author of *Think and Grow Rich*, intensely focusing on a single objective is the starting point for achieving all success, money, and happiness you desire.

This concept has changed millions of people's lives and will continue to transform even more lives in the future. It's time you embrace this idea as well. It's a major step forward in increasing your productivity.

"You must be single-minded. Drive for the one thing on which you have decided." – **George S. Patton Jr.**, the renowned American general who commanded troops in the United States Army during WWI and WWII.

Summary

- In today's work culture, multitasking is perceived as being productive.

- Studies have proven that multitasking can reduce your productivity by up to 40 percent!

- A much better alternative is to select ONE task that needs to be done. Work on it with your complete attention until it gets done. Then, move to the next task.

- It might *look* slower than multitasking on the surface, but there'd be a noticeable improvement in both the quality and quantity of your work.

72. Apply The "80/20" Rule

The Problem

How many times have you been in a situation where you have a long list of things to do and not enough time and energy? The sheer number of tasks feel too daunting to tackle. Hence, you start hesitating to take any action at all.

The Procrastination Solution

This is where the 80/20 rule comes into the picture.

Recommended by productivity experts around the world, the 80/20 rule is also called the "Pareto Principle" as it was named after the Italian economist Vilfredo Pareto. The 80/20 rule suggests that 80% of your results come from 20% of your activities.

For instance, suppose you have ten things on your to-do list. Usually, two out of these 10 tasks will be worth more than the other 8 tasks - **combined!** The 80/20 rule allows us to identify these critical tasks and make them our number one priority.

Please note that the 80/20 ratio is not a fixed number. It could be something else like 60/40, or 70/30. More than the actual ratio, the key idea is that *a large portion of your results come from a small portion of your activities. Do these tasks first*.

For instance, 15% of a company's products produce 90% of total sales. Notice the difference? While the actual ratio is different from 80/20, it is still supporting the idea that the majority of sales are coming from a small number of products. The organization should focus more on those products.

That is the key essence of the 80/20 principle.

How to Apply the 80/20 Rule?

Here's how to utilize the 80/20 rule for productivity:

Step 1 – Write down the ten things that you have to do today. Then ask yourself this question – "If I could only accomplish one of the things that are on the list, which one would have the biggest positive impact?"

Step 2 – Use the question above again to find your second most important task.

At this point, you'll have identified the 20 percent of your tasks that would benefit you more than anything else. These two are your top priority and should be finished first.

Step 3 – After you are done with these two, you could begin working on other tasks as you see fit.

As simple as it might look at the first glance, the 80/20 rule has the potential to skyrocket your productivity by highlighting the few critical tasks that must be done. When you don't have a mountain of tasks in front of you, it becomes easier to overcome procrastination and spring into action. Once you begin applying the 80/20 rule and see the improvements in productivity, you'd never look back.

"To change your life, you need to change your priorities." – **Mark Twain**, American writer, humorist, publisher, and lecturer.

Summary

- Do you have a long list of tasks but not enough time & energy?

- The 80/20 rule lets you identify and focus on a few key activities that produce the biggest results.

- The key idea is that a large portion of your results come from a small portion of your activities. Do these tasks first.

- Use the three-step process above to identify your critical tasks and get them done quickly.

- Once you cut through the noise and focus on a few *key* activities, it becomes easy to spring into action and produce excellent results.

73. Strategic Delegation Of Nonessentials

The Problem

Do you feel stressed and overburdened with work? It's a common problem today. Whether you work alone or with a team, overburden is a real issue.

When you are good at your job, people like to assign more tasks to you. While it might not bother you at first, it can quickly increase your to-do list.

The truth is, you cannot do everything yourself. That's a fact. There is no such thing as a lone wolf when it comes to achieving real success. You need other people. If you truly want to be successful in your endeavors, you need other people's expertise.

The Procrastination Solution

This is where delegation comes in. It's a popular solution to reduce some workload from yourself. Whenever you ask somebody, *"what would you do to reduce workload*?" Usually, the first answer they give - is to delegate work.

People prefer it for a reason. There are quite a lot of benefits of delegating your work.

The most apparent benefit is lightening your workload. You transfer some of your responsibilities to others. That reduces the number of tasks you have to do and frees up your time, which is incredibly valuable as time is the most precious resource. We can always make more money, get fit again, get our relationships back, but we cannot get back any lost time.

So, it's the most precious resource we have, and delegation allows us to have more of it. That's significant.

The second benefit is that delegating work can help improve the skills of other people. In many cases, those people get a chance to tackle unique challenges and learn something new. It can result in skill and knowledge development, therefore, making it a win-win for both of you.

Third, if the person is already quite skilled at the work you are delegating, it can raise the quality of the outcome. If you can do a good job of it yourself, but the other person can do an exceptional job at the same thing, it would be wise to let them handle it. Your workload will get reduced, and the quality of the work will be improved. What more could we ask for?

So, these were some of the main benefits of delegating your work. It's an effective strategy, but we need to keep some things in mind before handing over responsibilities. Let's go over them in detail.

How to Delegate Your Work?

Delegation might look easy at the surface, but it's not that simple. Here are some guidelines to follow:

1. The first thing is to determine whether someone else is fit for the job? Would they be able to handle the task? What is their experience? What are their skills? What are their job responsibilities?

2. Next, find out if that person can work on your task? What is their current workload? Be careful not to overburden them too as it might result in poor quality or unnecessary delays.

Once you have decided that a person is fit for the assignment, here are the next steps:

3. Clearly tell them what are the desired outcomes. What do you want from them? Define the goal and deadlines. Let them know about any completion milestones. They should have a 100% clear picture of what needs to be done and when.

4. Clearly define their responsibilities and constraints. Let them know what they can and cannot do? Give them the scope of their authority.

5. Be careful to delegate tasks that are equal to or below their authority level. It is never a good idea to let someone handle a task that is above their authority level. For instance, would you authorize a junior finance executive to develop the financial strategy for the company? Try to match the task with their authority level.

6. Mention that they should try their best to resolve any problem that might come up. But they can come to you for support if they get stuck with a problem and can't seem to find a solution.

7. After you delegate the work, don't be too concerned with how it is being done. You should be focused on the end result. If you keep asking the person about every little step, it's a waste of their time and yours.

8. Let them know about the potential benefits of taking on new responsibilities, like improvements in knowledge and skills, more recognition, and possible growth opportunities.

These are some of the general guidelines that should be followed when delegating the assignment to someone else.

Overall, delegation is an excellent strategy to reduce your workload. If you frequently find yourself too busy or stressed at work, try it out. It might be the one strategy that ends up making all the difference for you.

"If you want to do a few small things right, do it yourself. If you want to do great things and make a big impact, learn to delegate." – John C. Maxwell, **American author, speaker, and pastor**.

Summary

● It's a common problem today to feel stressed and overburdened with work.

● Delegating tasks to others may be a popular solution for reducing some of your workload.

● Delegating work can make other people learn new things. On the other hand, delegating to experts results in higher quality output.

● Following the provided guidelines to transfer obligations smoothly.

74. Process-Centric Fixation

The Problem

It seems natural to focus on the 'end' results, the bigger picture, the rainbow behind the mountain. It feels amazing to think about how we would feel when we achieve our goals. From living a luxurious lifestyle to having a spiritual awakening, thinking about our desired outcome feels incredible.

But that approach is far from ideal. Why? Because 'end' results usually seem too daunting to achieve, especially at the beginning. If we do not have a plan of action, the 'end' results could overwhelm our motivation, and thus, we start procrastinating.

The Procrastination Solution

If we focus our attention less on the results and more on executing the plan of action, we'd learn faster, become more efficient, and procrastinate less.

For instance, suppose you want to obtain A+ grades in your upcoming exams. The process is quite simple; once you've decided on a chapter to study, you sit down, go through the material - page by page, taking notes till the chapter is finished. By following this simple plan of action daily, a student can maximize their chances to get A+ grades in the exams. The complicated goal of obtaining A+ grades is relatively simple in execution when you focus on the process instead of the outcome.

This concept applies to any kind of goal, from *"lose five pounds in 30 days"* to *"achieve the sales target."* Goals provide the overall direction, but they don't define a specific course of action. By becoming process-oriented, you carve out a step-by-step plan and focus on its execution. Having an end goal is nice, but focusing on the process is ultimately what gets you the result.

Key idea: Turn *"End goal"* into *"plan of action."*

Here are some examples:

"Study chapter six" becomes *"study chapter six for 3 hours today without distractions."*

"Achieve the sales target" turns into *"make 30 cold calls today."*

"Lose five pounds in 30 days" becomes *"replace oily, sugar-filled food with green vegetables."*

"Become more present" turns into *"meditate for 20 minutes every day."*

I positively believe that process orientation is a cure-all. To achieve the end result, we have to keep our heads down and follow the process. Having goals is great, but process orientation is the holy grail of all achievement. By focusing on the process, you start making progress and end up reaching your goals, sometimes even without realizing it.

> *"Taking massive action is living a few years of your life like most people won't, so that you can spend the rest of your life like most people can't."* – Unknown.

Summary

- Focusing on the end goal is a double-edged sword. End results usually seem too intimidating to achieve, especially at the beginning. It can make us second-guess ourselves.

- Goals provide the overall direction, but they don't define a specific course of action.

- A better approach would be to focus less on the results and more on executing the plan of action.

- A process-oriented approach is ultimately what gets you the result.

75. The Secret To Deep, Laser-Like Focus

The Problem

It's easy to get demoralized when you see how much work you have to do. You start doubting whether you can ever finish the work required to achieve the goal.

This kind of thought reduces your motivation, and you start procrastinating. This was a HUGE problem I faced every time I went after a big goal. After working with clients, I found that it's not only me, but everyone is facing the same problem.

After much trial and error, I found an effective solution to this problem.

The Procrastination Solution

Focus on doing your *current task* as best as you can and have faith that you did the best possible thing you could do for obtaining your goal in the future.

That's it! Just fully concentrate on your current action and do it in the best way possible. Don't think about the future goal, as it will distract you from your current task. Doing your best work *now* is the biggest step you can take towards your goal.

Leave the rest to faith. You did your part in the best way possible.

Now, sometimes you will feel overwhelmed again when you think about how much more you have to do. You will begin to question yourself - *"Is it worth it?"*, *"Am I doing it right?"*, *"Will it work?"*, *"Is my work good enough?"*

It can be scary and disheartening. But know the fact that doing your current task with 100% effectiveness is the *best possible thing* you can do, and it's the only variable you can control. No one else could have done anything more here. Even the most successful and productive people struggle with this from time to time.

That's the most anyone can do. So, be proud of yourself. You took the biggest possible step towards your goal.

Combine this with belief-building exercises mentioned in the last section to increase the conviction that you WILL reach your goal.

100% belief that you **will** succeed + Do your best at the current task = Massive Success!

> "*Don't stop when you are tired. Stop when you are done.*" - **Marilyn Monroe**, famous American actress, model, and singer.

Summary

- It's easy to get overwhelmed by seeing how much work you have to do.

- A great way to counter it is to adopt a "now" mindset.

- Focus on doing your *current task* as best as you can, and have faith that you did the best possible thing you could do for obtaining your goal in the future.

- Doing your best at the present task is the *only variable* that's under your control.

76. How To Use Task-Batching For Maximum Productivity

The Problem

We all have some routine tasks that are important but often missed because we couldn't find the time. These are your everyday tasks like cooking food, exercise, meditation, reading, washing dishes, mowing the lawn, etc. These are important but take a second seat to more important work like office projects, study, meeting deadlines, and creating content.

How do you manage time so that everything gets done?

The Procrastination Solution

The answer is to combine routine activities all together. Instead of tackling one at a time, we can complete two tasks in the same time frame.

Here are some effective combinations:

Example #1 – Audiobook + driving: Some people have a habit of reading before sleep. Here's an alternative. Instead of reading one chapter of a book before sleep, get the audiobook version and listen to it while driving, washing dishes, or mowing the lawn. It will free up precious time that can be used for other tasks.

Example #2 – Buying groceries + jogging/running/walking: If you go jogging every morning and are looking to save some time, here's an option. Instead of taking the car to the grocery shop, you could walk, jog, or run to buy your groceries.

Example #3 – Bicycle + office: If you really are short on time and don't have an hour to go to the gym or exercise at home, ride a bicycle to your office. It's a great way to add some exercise to your day.

Example #4 – Call friends & family + dinner: Getting in touch with friends & family is really important if you live alone in another city. We all are guilty of not contacting our loved ones enough. Here's a possible solution. Call your friends or family while you are preparing food. It'll hit two birds with one stone. You could even talk about the food that you're cooking and how tasty/healthy it is.

Example #5 – meditation + exercise: If you do meditation and exercise daily, you know how hard it is to do both every day consistently. Personally, I used to miss meditation more often. Then I combined meditation and exercise all together. Now I meditate for 10 minutes before doing my workout. Since I have started doing that, I never missed my meditation session. As a bonus, meditation calms my mind and makes me really present during my workout session.

These are just a few examples of what is possible when you combine routine tasks together. Since everyone's schedule is unique, try to come up with your own combinations to save time and energy.

With a bit of creativity, the sky is the limit with what you can mix together.

"Creative thinking is not a talent. It's a skill that can be learned. It empowers people by adding strength to their natural abilities, which improves teamwork, productivity, and profits." – **Edward De Bono**, Maltese psychologist, author, inventor, and philosopher.

Summary

- We all have some routine tasks that are important but often get missed because we couldn't find the time.

- The solution is to combine routine activities all together. Instead of tackling one at a time, we can complete two tasks at the same time.

- Use the examples mentioned above as a guide to come up with your own unique combinations.

Section VII
What To Do When You Are Facing Inner Resistance

The forthcoming techniques are related to removing your inner blocks to success that you may have. Most people have limiting beliefs that stop them from achieving the level of success they really desire. These beliefs can be formed due to many reasons – perhaps a traumatizing childhood experience, your parents, and your peer group, etc. Once created, they operate at the back of your mind for all time.

These limiting beliefs may block you from making progress in life. For example, whenever you see an opening for a better paying job, you may get thoughts flooding in that say - "I am not good enough" or "I'll apply next time".

The same applies to writing a book, growing your business, learning a new skill, etc. These limiting beliefs could be the reason behind your procrastination habit. If you are using techniques from the earlier chapters to overcome procrastination but are still struggling, then this section is for you.

A *Few* of these techniques are a bit controversial. Just note that some people swear by their effectiveness. Some say they don't work. We have tried to add scientific validation of the techniques wherever possible. They have worked amazingly well for us and the people we shared them with. That is why we wanted to share them with you. But, it is okay if you are not interested or are unsure.

Any new phenomenon is not taken seriously until it gets proven via advancements in technology. For example; in the past, scientists have said that an atom is the smallest particle in the universe. But later on, with the advancement in technology, they said an electron is the smallest particle in the universe. Recently, Quarks were discovered and crowned with the title "the smallest particle in the universe."

Scientists should perhaps say to cover this, "*based on the technology we have right now, Quarks seem to be the smallest particles in the universe.*"

Technology is constantly evolving and new ideas & concepts are being discovered all the time. So all we are asking is that, even though *some* techniques towards the end of the upcoming section (I.e., chapters 86 to 91) are not widely accepted by science (yet), please go through these techniques with an open mind. Try them out. They could be the missing link for you.

We believe in these ideas. They have made a positive impact on us and many others. They might do the same for you. Please give them a fair shot. You may be pleasantly surprised!

77. The Essential Rule Of Personal Conduct

The Problem

Some people rationalize that they are either lazy or not motivated enough. They just can't make themselves take action.

It's not always a motivation problem. The real issue could be *responsibility*. You have not taken full responsibility to go for what you want. You are still waiting for the right moment.

And it will never come... because the right moment to start moving towards your goals was five years ago. The next best moment is *right now*.

The Procrastination Solution

When you start taking full responsibility for everything that happens in your life, it will bring forth amazing changes. A study consisting of 40 participants shows that an average person who begins taking full responsibility for themselves reported a reduction in stress & hypertension and increased peace of mind.

Taking full responsibility not only helps in getting rid of your present issues, but it is also good for your mental and physical wellbeing.

Taking Full Responsibility

The first step is to decide what you want and what you don't want. Having clear distinctions of haves and have nots will allow you to focus in one direction entirely. Sometimes you are motivated by what you desire. Sometimes you are motivated to avoid a painful situation. Either one works. Become fully aware of your likes and dislikes.

Being aware helps you decide the course you are going to take. Whether you desire something - a new job, a mate, a better body, financial freedom, or you desperately want to avoid a difficult situation - Being broke, lonely, desperate, sick, overweight, you have to decide and find a path towards it.

Once you do decide what you want, you make the necessary effort to bring forth your desire. You focus on a goal for a period of time, cut out distractions, change your schedule, and be disciplined enough to work on it daily.

This persistence and mindset occur only after you take full responsibility for yourself. It gives you inner strength and resolve. It inspires you to take the right actions because you know it is all up to you. There is no one else to blame if things go wrong.

Do You Really Want It?

If you are not taking full responsibility to change something, it means you don't want it (or don't want it as much). Believe me, when something is important enough, you will do anything and everything to make it happen. You will have unlimited energy and motivation.

No procrastination. No laziness. No excuses. You will be relentless.

Examine yourself. Maybe you are not taking responsibility because you think your desire is not worth the effort. For instance, you may like to have six-pack abs, but it is not a high priority for you at this moment in time. You would love to have it, but it is not critically important. It is not a *must-have*.

This is good, actually. It saves you from unnecessary stress. There are hundreds of things we would love to have in our life, but they are not that urgent. Nice to have but not an absolute must.

Think about it. If you start stressing over all the things you want, you'll go crazy. That is why sorting out your priority goals is of such importance. Your priority goals are the ones you need to have in your life right now.

If you are having health issues, that is your priority goal. A trip to Paris can wait.

If you are in the middle of establishing a new business, a beach-ready body + tan can be put aside.

Whatever your goal is, make sure it is really yours. Don't make the mistake of following the golden standards set by media and television. Why? Because social standards created by media change frequently. Before you reach that standard, it will get changed to something else. And even if you do achieve standards set by TV and media, the happiness would be short-lived.

The second reason - even more important - is that they are not *your* goals. Only **you** get to decide what makes you happy. Following standards set by others can be a helpful starting point but, it will never bring you real fulfillment.

You will experience true happiness only when you are living a life that you think is worth living, not someone from the advertisement industry.

Don't buy into society's standards of how you should look and live your life. Whether big or small, go for the goals that you want. Define your value and live by them.

Once you decide what you want, carve out a path towards it. Make plans and execute non-stop.

This is the process of creating any change you want in your life... the only prerequisite is that you have to take full responsibility for yourself, your life, and your happiness.

And it all starts with a change in your self-talk.

> *"Have you noticed that most of your problems in life are due to the fact that you are listening to yourself instead of talking to yourself?"* – **Martyn Lloyd Jones**, Welsh Protestant minister.

Summary

- Procrastination is not always a motivation problem. The real cause could be *responsibility*.

- Changes happen when you start taking full responsibility for everything in your life.

- The first step is to decide what you want and what you don't want. Having clear distinctions of haves and have nots will allow you to fully focus in one direction.

- If you are not taking full responsibility to change something, it means you don't want it (or as much). Because when something is important enough, you will do anything and everything to make it happen.

78. Resistance Equals Priority

The Problem

Have you ever had any important work to do, and there were no visible obstacles that could stop you from doing it, but you still didn't do it? That's the work of inner resistance.

Resistance is the enemy of growth and achievement. It is an inner force that blocks us from making progress and achieving our objectives. Resistance wants us to stay the way we are. It wants to hold us at our place.

The Procrastination Solution

Resistance is a feeling inside us whose sole aim is to stop us from doing the right thing at the right time. It is important to note that the more important the work is for our personal, professional, or spiritual growth, the stronger the resistance we face.

For example, resistance does not affect us when engaging with low-priority activities like watching TV, chatting on social media, hanging out with friends. It arises only when we are doing something meaningful. If you are a writer, resistance will try to stop you from sitting down and writing. If you are a student, it will prevent you from studying. If you are a business owner, it will try to stop you from growing your business. It will always be there to stop us when we are working on our life mission, our true calling, our priorities.

Remember, the more important the task, the stronger the resistance.

What's the Point of This Knowledge?

Knowing the enemy is half the battle won. This was an introduction to the phenomenon of resistance. Before we dive into ways to overcome it, we should know what we are dealing with. The enemy is within us. It's a feeling that exists only to stop us from doing what's important.

In my personal experience, learning about resistance and how to overcome it had a profound impact on my health & professional life. I can't imagine what I would be doing if I didn't learn to deal with resistance. It changed my life, and now I want to share it with you.

The upcoming chapters will help you identify inner resistance and overcome it. The important thing is to be open-minded and give them all a fair shot. They might not be the most popular or research-proven like others, but they made a big difference in my life and in the lives of people that I have shared them with.

"Don't prepare. Begin. Our enemy is not a lack of preparation. The enemy is resistance, our chattering brain producing excuses. Start before you are ready." – **Steven Pressfield**, the author of War of Art.

Summary

- Inner resistance is an inner force that blocks us from making progress and achieving our objectives.

- It wants to hold us at our place.

- The more critical the task, the stronger the resistance.

- The more we are closer to finishing our work, the stronger the resistance we face.

- The upcoming segments will help you identify inner resistance and how to overcome it.

79. Identification Of Internal Impediments

The Problem

Between you and the goal you want to accomplish, there is usually one major challenge blocking you, and it's hidden from your perception. In order to achieve your goal, you must be able to identify and then overcome that roadblock.

The Procrastination Solution

To uncover the inner resistance, find a quiet & peaceful environment (usually the bedroom) and ask yourself the below questions:

"Why achieving (insert your goal) is bad?"
"Am I capable enough to achieve (insert your goal)?"
 "Why do I think that I am not good enough?"
"Why am I not living my dream life right now?"
"Will I be able to handle success if I achieve my goal?"

Ask questions like these and allow the answers to come up. You'll be shocked to find the things that come up. Most of the time, you'll uncover limiting beliefs from childhood & early adolescent period. During childhood and early adolescent period, our brain is like a sponge. It is constantly absorbing all the information bombarded on us and trying to make sense of it. In pure innocence, our mind creates limiting beliefs that hinder us constantly in our adult life.

The above exercise is a great way to uncover these hidden limiting beliefs that are still blocking us from moving ahead in life. Once you identify the barrier, focus all your attention on eliminating it. This can significantly boost your productivity and overall level of success.

If your business is not at the level where you want it to be, examine your personal limiting beliefs first because your business is a reflection of you. When you are constrained, it will show up in your business. By removing your own barriers, you give your business a chance to reach its maximum potential.

Whether your business is having issues in sales & marketing, or finance, or product development, all of these are symptoms of the core issue – you. When you free yourself from your personal challenges, every issue in your business will get sorted out.

Note: We will cover the process of changing beliefs in the upcoming segments.

Identifying and then eliminating your personal constraints usually provides the biggest jumps in productivity and performance more than any other single activity. It fills you up with energy and drive. Once you free yourself, success is sure to follow.

"Whether you think you can, or think you can't, you are right." –
Henry Ford, American business magnate and founder of the Ford Motor Company.

Summary

- There might be some limiting beliefs behind your procrastination habit that are blocking you from achieving your goals.

- We must identify and then overcome those inner barriers.

- Use the above-mentioned exercise to uncover limiting beliefs.

- We will cover the process of changing beliefs in the following segments.

80. The Language Of The Brain

The Problem

Most of us spend a lot of time inside our mind — worrying about the future, replaying events in the past, and generally focusing on the parts of life that that leave us dissatisfied. These unwanted thoughts can distract you from focusing on what's important and reduce productivity.

The good news is that with dedicated practice, you can replace negative thinking patterns with thoughts that actually help. This can make an enormous difference in your ability to overcome procrastination.

The Procrastination Solution

Several pieces of research have proven that the brain can change itself well into the later years of adulthood. This phenomenon is called *Neuro-Plasticity*. Every thought we think, every conscious or subconscious thought we say to ourselves, is translated into electrical signals which, in turn, control the emotions we feel, the words we say, and the actions we take.

We program our brain with our *self-talk*.

It is the language of the brain.

Self-talk presents a way to *override* our past negative programming by using direct, specific positive commands.

With self-talk, we have a way to affect our subconscious mind by using different words and statements, which are more effective and helpful in improving any targeted area of life.

It lets you take charge of your life. It makes you feel in control.

Just like forming any other habit, it will take some repetition to attain a permanent place in your mind. We will begin with a concise, direct language that affects our thoughts, which eventually affects the emotions we experience and the actions we take.

And the first step is to *decide* that you are going to use the right language that will reshape your brain.

Thousands of people like you have used ideas like these to completely rewire their mindset and change their circumstances for the better.

The reality we experience is based on how we *perceive* our surroundings and situation. Our perception creates our reality. What you *want* to see is what you *do* see. What you *want* to hear is what you *do* hear.

And our perception depends on the kind of self-talk we do. If you use the right language at the right moments, you will observe that things feel different. The situation might not be extremely favorable, but you would feel different.

Your focus would shift to what you can do to improve it. This shift in perception would feel effortless, and you would subconsciously start moving towards *what you want* instead of *what you don't want*.

The language of the brain

How do we do it? How can we use self-talk to change the non-stop conversation going inside our heads?

We use the *right kind of language*.

In other words, we use definite and concise statements meant to penetrate deep inside our minds. Using the language of such power cuts through all mental chaos and gives control to your hands.

Definite and concise language means using wishy-washy, uncertain language is a big no-no. There is no "*I am going to try*" or "*I think I should do that*" or "*Maybe I should do that*." Using such weak language is like creating a huge roadblock in your mind.

When you talk to yourself in such language, the mind says, *"nope! It is not important right now."*

The keyword here is *right now*.

Your mind keeps your desires (stated in weak language) aside for later because it believes it's not very important at the present moment.

You want to tell your mind, "hey…, listen to me. This is important. Pay attention now!" This is done by using definite and concise language. When you use the right words, your brain will stop thinking about what will happen in the next episode of Game of Thrones and listen to you.

Using definite and concise language like "I am…" or "right now, I accept…" or "I am becoming…" puts emphasis on *changes happening at the present moment*. Not in the distant future. Your mind takes it way more seriously.

For example, say, "*I am going to become a good person*." Notice how that feels.

Not very inspiring, eh?

Now say, "*I am a good person*."

How did that feel?

Think about it. When you use weak language, you don't feel much of an impact even when words are coming out of your mouth. Why will your subconscious mind take it seriously? It will just ignore the statements because there is no power or impact in those words.

You can rewire your brain profoundly by using definite and concise language on a daily basis. The changes you can experience will be amazing, and it only requires that you change the old, defeating self-talk with definite and concise language that will empower you.

The only real requirement is *consistency*. Any habit or change requires daily practice. You must follow the process for at least a month so that it allows new neural pathways to develop inside your brain.

It will get easier and easier as time passes. Eventually, empowering self-talk will become an automatic habit. You have to experience that feeling. It will be one of the most fulfilling things you would ever experience.

> *"You have been criticizing yourself for years through self-talk, and it hasn't worked. Try approving yourself and see what happens."* – **Louise Hay**, American motivational author.

Summary

- Negative thoughts can distract you from focusing on what's important and reduce productivity.

- We program our brain with our *self-talk*. It is the language of the brain.

- When we repeat definite and concise statements to ourselves, they penetrate deep inside our minds.

- Conversely, the mind ignores weak language because there is no power behind those words.

81. Reinforce Constructive Behavior Patterns

The Problem

A lack of belief is often an underlying cause of procrastination.

In our daily life, we are constantly bombarded with countless messages from media like TV, social media, newspapers, and magazines that we are not good enough; we'll never be as good as "them," we can't have that, etc.

Do you remember the TV commercial with a young, handsome guy with six-pack abs surrounded by six girls, or a female model with a perfect figure walking down the red carpet, or a celebrity arriving at a hot party in his Lamborghini?

Social media, in particular, is filled with pictures and videos of people traveling the world, showing off their multimillion-dollar apartment and seven Ferrari's.

While being completely harmless on the surface, this kind of exposure creates self-doubt in an average person. It subtly creates a "standard" in people's minds that they believe they cannot reach. When we are constantly reminded of our shortcomings, self-doubt starts to creep in our minds. It gives birth to a 'lack of self-belief' and may stop you from taking action.

The Procrastination Solution

A great way to counter it, is to actively reinforce positive beliefs that empower you.

There are several ways to reinforce positive beliefs. My personal favorite is affirmations. Affirmations are positive statements that you repeat again and again to fill your mind with absolute certainty.

Affirmations act as a daily reminder of your capabilities and your value as a person. It will be your daily "boost" of confidence. It will protect your confidence against all sorts of nonsense thrown at you.

Widely successful people like Oprah Winfrey, Will Smith, Jim Carrey, Arnold Schwarzenegger repeatedly mentioned the effectiveness of affirmations.

Affirmations really do work, but you have to use them correctly. I have been doing affirmations for years now, and I can honestly say they made a significant positive impact on my life.

How to Do Affirmations Correctly?

Step 1. Write down your doubts and insecurities on a piece of paper. Then, identify five of your *biggest* doubts and insecurities which you believe are holding you back the most. Refer to the "Identify what's blocking you" part for a step-by-step guide.

Step 2. After you have identified five of your biggest limiting beliefs, write down their exact opposite positive statement. For example, if your doubts statement is "*I don't deserve to be rich,*" then its opposite positive statement could be "*I fully deserve to be rich.*"

Change all five of your doubts into their opposite positive statements. Write them down on paper.

Note: Make sure all your affirmations are positive and in the present tense. Don't make affirmations for the future, like "*I will succeed in the future,*" "*I will have a fit body,*" etc. Your mind puts these statements in the "maybe-in-the-future" category.

Your affirmations must be positive and in the present tense. For example, I am successful. I deserve to be rich. I have a fit body. I have abundance in my life, and so on.

Positive and present tense.

Step 3. After you have converted your five negative beliefs into positive ones on paper, write down another five positive beliefs which you believe will help you the most. These five beliefs are the mindset that you would want to have. For example, I am a good learner, I can deal with any situation, etc.

Step 4. You now have ten affirmations that you would like to have as beliefs. Five positive ones converted from your negative beliefs, and another five ones you think are great to have. It's time to install these ten beliefs in your mind. Stand in front of a mirror (preferably full length where you can see your whole body) and look *directly* into your eyes.

Step 5. Say your affirmations out loud three times. Make sure to say them with PASSION & EMOTION, like you really believe them. You can use your facial expressions and gestures to bring up the emotions while saying your statements. This is very important.

For instance, if your affirmation is, "*I am enough,*" say it like you *really* mean it! Change your posture. Stand tall, chest forward like you are proud of yourself. Put both of your hands up and shout "YESSSS!" in a triumphant voice. FEEL the emotion and passion in your voice.

Do whatever you can to bring emotion into your affirmations. Statements mixed with emotions have a deep penetrating effect on our minds.

Anthony Robbins (success coach, author of *'Unlimited Power'* & *'Awaken The Giant Within'*) and Dr. Joseph Murphy (author of *'The Power Of Your Subconscious Mind'*) have also stressed the importance of mixing emotion into your affirmations. Without it, you would be doing affirmations for years without much benefit.

Do your affirmations daily. It's a great way to build new positive beliefs. It only takes about five minutes, and within two to three weeks, you'll start noticing changes in your behavior. Over time, these positive statements will become a permanent part of your persona.

Summary

- Limiting beliefs are often the underlying cause of procrastination.

- Affirmations are positive statements that you repeat daily to fill your mind with absolute certainty.

- Use the five-step process above to build positive beliefs using affirmations.

- When repeated daily, these positive statements become a permanent part of your mindset.

82. Accumulating References Of Productive Events

The Problem

If you take any kind of action without the necessary self-beliefs, it would be like driving a car with the handbrakes on. It results in a lot of wasted energy.

You want to have your beliefs help you move forward, not slow you down. When you believe you can, then you are halfway there! Once you win the battle in your mind, you will almost certainly achieve it in the real world.

The Procrastination Solution

One of the most powerful ways to weaken your limiting beliefs while simultaneously strengthening a positive belief is to DELIBERATELY collect references for it.

To do this, think about two or three positive beliefs that will benefit you the most. These are the beliefs that you believe will be most helpful to have in your present situation. Now, take a new diary and write these beliefs down on the first page.

This is your table-top or the beliefs you want to have. Now you need to collect references (real-life evidence) to support your selected beliefs.

Your subconscious mind (where the beliefs are stored) does not care about logic. It never debates whether something is RATIONAL or not.

If you provide enough references, it will believe ANYTHING! You have the potential to have any belief you want in your life.

Now, as you go about your day, keep an eye out for anything which could even REMOTELY support your selected beliefs. For instance, if one of your selected beliefs is "*I am becoming a productive person*," then references to support that belief from your daily life could be:

a) I am always on time. A productive person is punctual. I am a productive person.

b) I worked the best I could today, just like a productive person. I have what it takes.

c) I want to be a productive person, and I am working in that direction.

Let's take another example. Say your belief is, "*I CAN change myself to become a more positive person.*"

As you go about your day, consciously try to look at things in a more positive light. Even the smallest of incidents where you had a positive thought counts as a reference of belief - "*I CAN change myself to become a more positive person.*"

A very important part is writing down these references on a piece of paper or even on your mobile phone notepad. You are creating a written list of "references." Do not underestimate the power of written words.

When you go to sleep at night, take out your list of references you made during the day and look at it for a few minutes. Now you see REAL WORLD evidence of positive thoughts that came into your mind during the day. It MASSIVELY boosts your self-confidence and strengthens your belief "*I CAN change myself to become a more positive person.*"

In order to change, your mind craves proof (references) that you can become that type of person. And nothing could be more effective than a list of "real world" references that you collected during the day.

This reference list could be endless. It only requires little creativity and a positive approach. Any small, trivial thing could be your reference. You could even change the meaning of something negative and view it as a reference for your empowering beliefs.

For instance, you want to start your own business but are doing a 9-to-5 job to pay your bills. If you are feeling bad about the current situation, you can change its meaning from "*this is such a horrible situation. I am stuck here.*" to "*You know what? This horrible experience is the universe's way of forcing me to work harder towards my goal: to create my own business.*"

You can change the meaning of any situation and view it as a reference to strengthen your empowering beliefs. Many people do it subconsciously... but they do it to reinforce NEGATIVE beliefs such as "*people are mean,*" "*money is hard to come by,*" or "*I am lazy.*"

You will do it consciously... for the positive ones. As you find (or create) references during the day, write them down immediately on your phone, so you don't forget them. When you come home, WRITE THEM DOWN in your diary as "evidence for belief..."

Writing down your thoughts on paper works like magic. It penetrates deep into your mind. Your collected references will create a deep sense of certainty about your selected belief.

As you continue to collect references for your beliefs, within just 4-5 days, you will start feeling different. The belief will begin to feel VERY REAL.

If you continue to gather references for your empowering beliefs (which you should), they will become so ingrained in your mind that nothing will ever shake them out. You'll have rock-solid beliefs for the whole life.

> *"The only limits you have are the limits you believe."* – **Wayne Dyer**, American spiritual author and speaker.

Summary

- Any action without the necessary self-beliefs results in a lot of wasted energy.

- An excellent way to build positive beliefs is to DELIBERATELY collect references for it.

- If you provide enough references, your subconscious mind will believe anything.

- As you go about your day, keep an eye out for anything which could even REMOTELY support your selected beliefs.

- Review your collected references before sleep. Note it down.

- As you continue to gather references for your empowering beliefs, they will become ingrained in your mind forever.

83. A Guide To Overcome Failure & Rejection

The Problem

We are afraid of failure, rejection, and disappointment. Thoughts like "*It won't work?*", "*I am not good enough,*" and "*I have never achieved something like this before*"; race through our minds when we start pursuing a significant goal.

It's very common to experience thoughts like that, especially when we go after a goal that is beyond our past achievements. It can hinder your productivity and results.

But what if I tell you that you can ENSURE your success one hundred percent, and there is no such thing as a failure?

The Procrastination Solution

Contrary to what people may believe, failure is not the end of the road to success. Failure is an indicator that you need to try something different to obtain your goal. You need to change your approach; do something different if your current plan is not working, and keep trying out different approaches/plans/actions until you find something that works.

For instance, suppose you are trying to get in shape. You're going to the gym six times a week and following a healthy diet plan but still not able to lose weight. Instead of getting disheartened, collect more information - consult your dietitian, read the best books on weight loss, etc.

Find out how the human body works, how we put on fat, and how fat is converted into energy. Find out different forms of exercises like high-intensity interval training, cross-fit, etc. New information would show you several different ways to lose weight.

Pick any one. Make changes in your diet and exercise routine and continue it for a month or two. Look for the progress. If you don't see any improvement, make changes in your diet and exercise program yet again.

Stick to it, and look for the results. Rinse and repeat until you find a diet & exercise plan which works for you.

Success is virtually GUARANTEED if you keep trying different approaches to obtain your objective. The ONLY way you cannot succeed is when you CHOOSE to stop trying.

Success is like finding the combination of a lock. You may need to try a few different combinations, but if you persist, you'll eventually get the lock open. Persistence, when combined with changing your approach, is the recipe for guaranteed success.

Some people may ask, "*But how do I find other approach options? How would I know what to try next?*"

We live in an age where information is available at every moment. There are thousands of books, eBooks, YouTube videos, seminars, audio programs, blogs, newsletters, CD and DVD programs, podcasts, and other sources available to you right now. Take advantage of them.

Most successful and productive people in the world are constant learners. They never stop learning. Bill Gates was a college dropout who became one of the richest people in the world. He attributes the majority of his success to being a constant learner.

Research repeatedly shows that learning and constantly improving yourself are more powerful predictors of success than a college degree. According to a research paper co-published by Nobel Prize-winning economist James Heckman, it has been found that personality is one of the strongest predictors of success. Personality traits like self-discipline, perseverance, diligence are vital for being successful. On the contrary, IQ only accounts for 1-2% of income differences.

Link to research:
http://ftp.iza.org/dp10356.pdf

While it's great to have a college degree, you need to become a student of life.

Whatever your challenges might be, if you look for a solution, you will find it. Look around; it always amazes me that we can get millions of dollars' worth of information in a $10 soft-cover book!

Incredibly successful people, who have spent their lifetime overcoming challenges, shared their experience and knowledge in a little book, and you have access to it! You are fortunate enough to learn what they learned in about a fraction of the time it took them to discover these ideas.

We are blessed to live in times like this. Think about it. You have a massive advantage over previous generations, which didn't have the kinds of resources available to you now.

Learn and use this knowledge. You can discover several options to reach your destination. Pick any one, and start taking action. Look for progress and make changes if needed.

> *"I can accept failure. Everyone fails at something. But I can't accept not trying."* - **Michael Jordan**, American basketball legend.

Summary

• The fear of failure, rejection, and disappointment can hinder your productivity and results.

• Failure is only feedback. It is an indicator that you need to change your approach.

• Try a new approach. If it doesn't work out, try another one. Keep trying different approaches/plans/actions until you find one that works.

• Success is virtually GUARANTEED if you keep trying different approaches to obtain your objective. The ONLY way you can't succeed is when you CHOOSE to stop trying.

84. Enhancing Immunity To Unfair Criticism

The Problem

We want to avoid criticism however we can. In fact, the majority of the decisions we make are influenced by criticism. If an endeavor has the potential to expose us to criticism, we try to evade it. Most of our daily behaviors are shaped by criticism, especially when it comes to our work.

Facing criticism is an uncomfortable feeling. Thus, we try our best to avoid activities that might expose us to it. The more the chances of being criticized, the less interested we are in pursuing a task. But is that good for us? Most of the time, any significant goal or achievement will attract its fair share of criticism. That's how success works. Criticism is the price you pay for having ambition. If you decide not to do something based on whether you'd get criticized or not, it can hold you back from achieving the results you want.

We need to get over criticism. We need to make sure that it doesn't stop us by influencing our decision to take action.

The Procrastination Solution

Here's the truth - 99% of the time, how people behave is not about you. It's about them. Their behavior depends on a long list of underlying reasons. And even if you are on that list, you probably rank at the very bottom. There are several reasons that determine other people's behavior, and most of the time, they are not related to you at all. When someone criticizes you, be wary of the impulse to win their approval. Their disrespect is not a valuation of your worth. It is a signal of their character.

I cannot stress enough how important this is for you socially. If you do not internalize that people's behavior has nothing to do with you, you can never be truly free as far as your social life is concerned. Often people don't realize the price you paid to get to where you are today. They just don't. And if you let each and every little comment shake you up, it's not healthy for your emotional health & self-confidence.

Let's look at an example. If a cashier in your bank acts rudely, you feel bad. That's pretty normal. You are a human being, and it is perfectly all right to feel bad if somebody misbehaves with you. BUT when you go home RAGING and think about that incident for hours… THAT is not normal.

It's a cue that you need to learn about not take things personally.

People Live in Their Own Reality

By going with the cashier example above, you repeat that incident in your head again & again, each time, feeling increasingly worse. Along with your hatred towards that person, you might start to think about the REASONS for which they behaved in that way.

Now comes the crucial part… Because you do not have any more information about them, you put the entire blame on yourself. And these thoughts have a vicious cycle. Thoughts, generally, start from *"maybe I said something bad"* to *"I always say something bad"* to *"I am not a good person"* to *"I deserved it!"*

These thoughts are harmful to you. They hurt you on various levels – Your self-confidence, self-worth, emotional health, physical health, and your happiness. Look at the criticism objectively. If it is constructive, learn from it. Otherwise, let it go.

Stop letting people who do so little for you control so much of your mind, feelings, and emotions. Remind yourself time and time again that other people have many underlying problems that are not apparent on the surface. If you could see what they are going through in their life, your hatred would turn into sympathy.

Maybe that cashier was having chronic back pain, making them irritating & rude, or perhaps they had a divorce yesterday afternoon, and their family life is in ruins. There could be a million reasons for their behavior that are not related to you at all.

Nothing others do is because of you. What they say or do is a reflection of their own reality, their own life. It says nothing about you but a LOT about them.

How can you be sure of what is going on in other people's heads at any point in time? People will love you. People will hate you. And most of the time, it will have nothing to do with you.

Objective reality is an illusion. People live in their own little world and only see what they want to see. You will be shocked to find the number of times people are focused on themselves. You might think people are looking at you and judging your every move, but in reality, people are caught up in their own little bubble. Everybody is looking at the world from a different set of eyes.

Nothing is good or bad. It all depends on the situation and each person's perspective. Whatever you believe will seem to be true. You cannot control any other person and/or their outlook. You can only control yourself. I suggest you deliberately try to find the good in everything.

Why?

Because life is just too short to live in misery and blame everything. Life goes faster than you think. Ask anyone in his fifties or sixties about how fast they felt decades went by. The answer is always the same – *"pretty fast!"* So, love, laugh and try new things. Time will pass away. You can either spend it creating the life you want or spend it living the life you don't want. The choice is yours.

> *"No one can make you feel inferior without your consent."* – **Eleanor Roosevelt**, American former first lady, diplomat, and activist.

Summary

• Never blame, complain, and take things personally. Instead, focus on the more important things in your life, things which you are grateful for. Enjoy the little things in life because one day, you will look back and realize they were the big things.

• If somebody makes a sly comment on you or behaves rudely, brush it off. It's not about you. Think BIG and don't listen to people who tell you that it is impossible. When someone tells you it can't be done, it's more a reflection of their limitation, not yours.

• Look at the criticism objectively. If it is constructive, learn from it. Otherwise, it is always better to forget and move on. Not everyone will understand your journey. That's ok. You are here to live your life, not to make everyone understand. It's no use trying. People will love you. People will hate you. And most of the time, it will have nothing to do with you.

85. Disregard Of Perpetual Demoralization

The Problem

Naysayers can rob us of our energy and enthusiasm. It can cause us to question our decisions and become hesitant to take action. While we may not be able to avoid all naysayers, maintaining a healthy distance from constant criticism can lead to positive results.

The Procrastination Solution

Do your best to surround yourself with positive people. Pay attention to how they talk, what they say, and how they think. Expose yourself to the company of positive people as much as possible.

It is a psychological fact that we become a combination of five people with whom we spend most of our time. By being around successful, positive, and grateful people, your mind will start adopting their behavior subconsciously. We absorb the thinking patterns of people around us, whether it is positive OR negative. That's the way our brains are wired.

> *"Associate yourself with people of good quality, for it is better to be alone than in bad company"* - **Booker T. Washington,** American educator and advisor to several presidents of the United States.

What to Do if You Can't Find Positive People Around You?

This is a genuine issue for many people. But here's the good news. Don't be discouraged if you can't find positive people to hang out with. I discovered that great books, audio, video, live programs, etc., all count towards changing your mind to be positive. It's not only about the surrounding people. It's about the top five "influences" that affect you daily.

Reading a book by someone who is massively successful will influence your mind to think like them. As you continually read, watch or listen to noteworthy individuals, you will gradually begin to adopt their beliefs and mindsets, which would be immensely helpful if you can't find people like that in your actual life.

One of the most significant advantages of having a positive mindset is that it changes your focus from "surviving" to "thriving." Have you noticed people who are just coping through life? Their motivation is to "get by." For them, having just enough to survive is FINE.

With the right company and the right mindset, you will see situations and people differently. Your focus will be on what's good and what's possible. You will have more passion and zest for life, which other people will instantly notice.

> *"The person who says it cannot be done, should not interrupt the one doing it."* – Chinese proverb.

Summary

- Stay away from naysayers, as they can rob us of our energy and enthusiasm.

- Conversely, expose yourself to the company of positive people as much as possible.

- We absorb the thoughts & behaviors of people we spend time with, whether positive OR negative.

- If you can't find positive people in your social circle, don't worry. Great books, audio, video, live programs, etc., all influence your mind to be positive.

86. Mitigating Turbulent Emotions

The Problem

Thoughts and emotions come and go like clouds in the sky. Sometimes it's sunny; sometimes it rains – sometimes you feel motivated; sometimes you feel lethargic.

If you're trying to finish your presentation slides, exercise, or do anything worthwhile, the likelihood is that that negative thoughts and emotions will crop up. You feel a way of hysteria, feel overwhelmed, feel stressed, and certainly won't feel motivated. Your mind is advising you to do the task tomorrow. That's when you'll desire it. That's when you'll be motivated. But as you know, it doesn't work like that.

Your mind is a reason-giving machine. It will rationalize anything that's just a little bit uncomfortable and create endless excuses for why you shouldn't do something right now. Those excuses are irrational but sound quite convincing at that moment.

We take them at their face value and end up postponing the task.

The Procrastination Solution

An effective way to manage your emotions is by practicing mindfulness. The Oxford dictionary defines mindfulness as 'a mental state achieved by concentrating on the present moment, while calmly accepting the feelings and thoughts that come to you, used as a technique to help you relax.'

Mindfulness is all about maintaining a non-judgmental, moment-by-moment awareness of whatever is happening in the present moment. This involves awareness of bodily sensations, thoughts, feelings, and therefore the surrounding environment. Non-judgment is essential because it entails acceptance, meaning that we pay attention to our thoughts and feelings without judging them. We can watch them without labeling them as "good or bad," "pleasant or unpleasant."

Mindfulness allows us to step back and watch our thoughts and emotions from a particular distance. It allows us to feel negative emotions without reacting to them.

Bringing it back to procrastination, mindfulness allows us to take action despite experiencing negative emotions. First, it raises our awareness of what's happening in our minds. Second, it lets us stick with negative emotions without identifying with them, giving us the chance to do the right thing, no matter how we're feeling.

According to the research paper published by Norman Farb from the department of psychology, University of Toronto, there is solid evidence that mindfulness helps in developing emotional regulation in the brain.

Link to study:
https://www.researchgate.net/publication/23452393

In another randomized controlled trial done by Elizabeth A. Hoge and her co-researchers, it was found that mindfulness has a beneficial effect on generalized anxiety disorder.

Link to study:
https://pubmed.ncbi.nlm.nih.gov/23541163/

And that's not everything that mindfulness will do for you. Research has shown that it'll make you happier, healthier, more self-compassionate, more self-disciplined, better at tuning out distractions, and far more - all things that are proven to lower procrastination.

How to Practice Mindfulness?

The practice of mindfulness has too many intricate details, ideologies, and forms and it wouldn't be fair to include them here. There are better resources and teachers for learning about mindfulness if you are interested. I recommended checking out the book "Mindfulness in Plain English" by Bhante Henepola Gunaratana. It's a wonderful introduction to mindfulness for beginners.

> *"Mindfulness gives you time. Time gives you choices. Choices, skillfully made, lead to freedom."* - **Bhante Henepola Gunaratana**, author of *Mindfulness in Plain English*.

Summary

- Turbulent emotions will cause you to delay taking action.

- The mind creates endless excuses that we take at their face value and end up postponing the task.

- Mindfulness is an effective way to manage your emotions.

- *"Mindfulness in Plain English"* by Bhante Henepola Gunaratana is an excellent introduction to the concept of mindfulness if you are a beginner.

87. Exploring The Therapeutic Effects Of Yoga For Productivity

Trapped Emotions in the Body: Emotional Blocks

Our body and emotions are more connected than we realize. Whenever we experience any intense negative emotions and don't allow the emotions to process the way they should, it gets stored in the body. For example, Emotional experiences like childhood trauma, physical or mental abuse, loss of a loved one, etc. are extremely taxing for an individual. Often, people suppress these emotions because they are difficult to deal with.

Over time, these suppressed emotions in our body turn into emotional blocks. They are like an invisible barrier that distorts our perception. These are usually buried in our subconscious mind and rise to the surface at different times.

Emotional blocks take a massive toll on our focus, self-worth, feelings of what we deserve and this puts a limitation on how successful we may become.

Its effects are not limited to just success and productivity. Over the long-term, suppressed emotions will cause deterioration in our overall health and can cause a number of physical & mental ailments. We cannot move forward in life if our emotions are stuck in the past, reliving old memories over and over. We need to let it go.

How Yoga Helps Release Emotional Blocks?

For centuries, some cultures have held beliefs that the mind, body, and soul are intrinsically linked, and one cannot treat an ailment as a single one without addressing all three.

Many cultures believe that mind and body are interconnected. We cannot heal one without addressing the other. Now, even science has acknowledged that the body has a direct effect on the mind.

Evidence of Mind-body connection:
https://www.ncbi.nlm.nih.gov/pmc/articles/PMC1456909/

Mind-body connection:
https://scholarworks.gsu.edu/cgi/viewcontent.cgi?article=1050&context=ssw_facpub/

Body map of emotions:
https://www.ncbi.nlm.nih.gov/pmc/articles/PMC3896150/

Resource: If you want more information on this subject, check out the book, *The Body Keeps The Score* by Bessel van der Kolk M.D.

My Personal Experience With the Mind-Body Connection

A long time ago, when I graduated from college and landed my first job, I was ecstatic. That was the plan. It was all that I wanted.

It was a huge firm and everybody wanted to be a part of it. I loved every minute of my job. Even though I was working on computers 8–9 hours straight, I was so happy.

After 6 months or so, I started experiencing pain in my lower back. I had never had any pain there before, so this was something new for me. I started sitting upright, thinking maybe poor posture could be the culprit.

It didn't help. The pain started getting worse... to the point where it became quite distracting. I couldn't focus on what I was doing.

So I went to a physician and after some tests, he told me that nothing was out of the ordinary. It was just a case of sitting all day that was causing the pain. He suggested a few back stretches along with some medicines and recommended that I join a gym.

I went straight to a gym near my apartment and enrolled. The next day, the gym instructor showed me around the set of beginner exercise machines. He told me that exercise would definitely help in lowering the back pain, but it would take some time.

I was fine with that concept as long as it would help in getting rid of that back pain. After a month or so of regular exercises, I noticed that my back pain didn't decrease, it actually increased.

That was a total shock to me! My doctors said everything is normal. Regular gym sessions under professional supervision were not helping. The pain kept getting worse and worse.

It was that moment I started panicking. "What is going on with me?" I wondered.

When something is getting worse and worse in your body and nobody is able to help, it gets very scary.

During my distressed state, I googled "how to cure back pain?" I got millions of websites stating different methods, ranging from using exotic exercises to aqua puncher.

It was all very confusing. However, I noticed yoga was coming up several times. I don't know why I decided to try yoga among all alternatives.

I quit my gym sessions and enrolled in a yoga class.

The first day I went to my yoga class, I didn't like it at all. The aroma, the peace & quiet (which I thought was a bit forced), and the postures... oh God! The postures were so difficult..... And this was a beginner's class.

My body just didn't bend the way everybody else's seemed to. My balance was non-existent and the instruction of putting attention on my breath while holding poses was out of this world.

I became totally exhausted within 20 minutes and it was an hour-long class. An hour later, it was like someone sucked the soul out of me. I went to the instructor and told him why I joined yoga but I felt that it wasn't for me. I wanted to cancel my enrollment.

He patiently listened to everything I had to say, then smiled and said, "Max, it is my request that you attend the class for one month. If you do not feel better, not only will we cancel your enrollment we will give you a full refund."

I was surprised by his confidence in yoga. He could have just canceled my enrollment and be done with it. But to offer a refund on top of that takes a lot of belief in his teaching.

So I decided to stick with it.

At first, it was beyond uncomfortable, to say the least. I always had terrible balance and zero flexibility. Getting into yoga postures and maintaining them for a few moments seemed more difficult than climbing a mountain with bathroom slippers on.

Whenever my instructor saw me having trouble with a posture (every posture actually), he came up to me, smiled and said, "Max, don't force it. Just do what your body is allowing you to do right now."

I had heard these words so many times that I would hear them in my sleep. I didn't push my body outside my comfort zone and slowly but steadily was able to flex my body a little more.

It was crazy but there was an improvement. By the end of the third week, I was able to flex my feet in a lotus posture. It's a sitting posture in which we cross both legs on top of each other. I was barely able to accomplish that but, it still counts as a big improvement. Earlier, even the thought of crossing one leg on top of another seemed like something out of fantasy land. I thought my naturally clumsy and stiff body was not made for yoga.

But I kept at it and within a month, I saw improvements in my flexibility and total balance.

The best part was that my back pain started decreasing from the second day of joining yoga. Before the end of the first month (during the fourth week to be exact), my back pain completely vanished!

I was surprised and very happy.

I couldn't believe it! What all those gym exercises, painkillers, medicines, and muscle relief creams weren't able to do; yoga did it in a few weeks.

I have done yoga ever since. Now I don't even sit in front of a computer all day, but I still do twenty minutes of yoga regularly.

There are multiple reasons behind it.

After my lower back pain disappeared, I got curious about why it happened. After reading a lot of books and articles on back pain and yoga, I found some very interesting information.

How Yoga Releases Unprocessed Emotions?

Back pain, especially lower back pain, is associated with experiencing a lot of stress. Recent researches on stress and trauma revealed that negative emotions, memories, and stress affect the body as much as the brain.

When we experience stress, our muscles tense up, especially around the lower back and pelvic region. The most important of all these muscles is the "Psoas Muscle." It is considered to be the fight or flight muscle of the body. It is connected to the base of our backbone, which goes all the way around and onto our nervous system on the other side.

Stress can cause Psoas and other muscles in the lower back and pelvic region to get stiff. This causes the stress response to reach our nervous system, which is connected to the backbone on the other end. It keeps the nervous system on high alert.

Notice that people who experience a lot of stress tend to react emotionally at the smallest of things? That's stress causing the nervous system to go into overdrive. It makes us "jumpy."

It's bad on several levels. Over time, it may lead to psychological disorders like depression and migraine, physical problems like mid or lower back pain, and could be detrimental to your immune system.

Yoga plays a big role here.

Yoga helps stretch out all major muscle groups of the body, more importantly, your core muscles, including the lower back and pelvic region.

Stretching causes muscle stimulation, which sends a different set of signals to the nervous system. Our brain receives these new signals and processes the negative memories and emotions differently. Think of it as the brain is sorting out a mess of tangled wires.

It shuts down the stress response and you start feeling relaxed. The nervous system calms down and the body feels relaxed.

You feel a sense of calmness, safety, and comfort. Fear, anxiety, and nervousness are drastically reduced.

Summary:

Unprocessed emotions will become stored in the body and may cause stress, anxiety, tension, lack of focus, and/or physical pain. Yoga is highly recommended for releasing these trapped emotions from the body. It can result in numerous physical and mental benefits including increased focus, energy, determination, and mental calmness - all quite useful for overcoming procrastination.

88. Trauma: What It Is, Why It Matters, And How To Heal It

How Does Past Trauma Affect You?

I have spent many years reading psychology literature, driven by my quest to find secrets of the human psyche. I had come across countless books and scholarly articles pertaining to different topics like mechanics of the subconscious mind, how habits work, perception, influence, and cognitive biases.

Out of all these fascinating topics, trauma stood out the most, largely because it was a relatively obscure subject. Not much was being talked about it in the mainstream media.

A lot of research done on trauma confirmed that it's a common underlying factor behind most of the behavioral problems like:

- Difficulty with concentration
- Bad memory
- Improper sleep patterns
- Most fears, anxiety, and phobias
- Relentless pursuit of perfectionism
- Chronic fatigue
- Repressed imagination & creativity
- Difficulties with habit formation and changing behavior
- Lack of motivation & self-confidence
- Hyper-focus

What's surprising is that both hyper-focus AND relentless pursuit of perfectionism - are common symptoms of trauma. On the surface, both look like a boon. But at closer examination, both are over-compensatory behaviors to cover up a weakness.

That means even productivity gurus that push the agenda of "non-stop hustle" or "80-hour workweek" should not be imitated blindly.

Could this single component be the cause of many common personal and professional issues? What does the science say? From a number of scientific researches on trauma, I recommend reading *"The Body Keeps The Score"* by Bessel van der Kolk M.D. It's a great introduction to trauma and its effects.

How the Trauma Gets Stored in the Body?

In the animal kingdom, when any animal gets attacked by a predator, its "fight or flight" response kicks into the body. If the animal is able to survive the attack and runs away to safety, it physically shakes the body to trigger the "safety" response.

It's a relatively unknown process for us because the threats we face, are not as obvious as a predator attack. Our threats are for instance: worrying about our finance, divorce, lawsuits, kid, health, competition at work, etc. It triggers a very low level of emotional response in our body that is barely noticeable but still affects our mind, body, and emotions.

One of the common signs of a stored "threat response" in the body is over-reaction to daily events. For example, do you feel "enraged" when the other car cuts in front of you while driving? Do you feel like yelling at the counter person if they made a mistake in your order? Do you get "furious" if someone cuts in front of you while waiting in line?

Anytime your emotional reaction to an event is higher than appropriate, it's a sign that there may be an unprocessed "threat response" in your body.

Link to research:
https://pubmed.ncbi.nlm.nih.gov/9384857/

A Solution to Let Go of the Trauma: TRE® Introduction

TRE® is a set of exercises that helps the body release stored trauma, tension, and stress. The exercise stimulates the body to trigger a natural reflex mechanism of "shaking".

When this natural shaking mechanism is triggered in a safe, comfortable environment, it results in lowered muscular tension and a calm nervous system. It can release a number of unprocessed emotions/memories stuck in the body, ranging from mild shyness to anger to severe panic attacks.

Here's a link to the TRE® website:
https://traumaprevention.com/

Disclaimer: *TRE® has not been evaluated by the US Food & Drug Administration or the American Medical Association. This technology is not intended to diagnose, treat, cure, or prevent any disease. Medical advice must only be obtained from a physician or qualified health practitioner. Results may vary between individuals. There are no guarantees, expressed, or implied.*

Personal Experience

I have personally tried TRE® and talked to a lot of people who have tried it. Almost everyone experienced a deep sense of relaxation. It lowered anxiety, reduced stress, and improved mood.

Reduced emotional reaction to negative events was a common occurrence. For example, one person said arguments with her co-workers in-office meetings used to stress her out so much that she was unable to convey her point-of-view. But after she started doing TRE®, she felt extremely calm & poised and was able to get her point across effortlessly.

Some people who practiced TRE® said they were able to laugh more freely. Even small jokes, that they didn't find funny before, would make them laugh aloud. Many reported mental relaxation and inner calm that sharpened their focus. They find that they can now concentrate on one task for long periods of time without getting distracted.

There were many smaller benefits like increased tolerance to opposing point of views, improved relationships at home & work, better sleep & waking up refreshed. All of these benefits are super important but we will mostly focus on this one: almost all people experienced a boost in productivity. They were able to get more things done during the day. Heightened focus, arising from a relaxed mind, resulted in overall better performance at their job, business, and studies.

Give TRE® a shot if you want. If you are not interested in TRE®, look for other alternatives to release trauma. There are a number of studies being done on trauma and how it affects us. It is such an important and overlooked aspect of our lives. If left unresolved, it can stop us from achieving all the success and happiness that we want and deserve.

You can find some great books available on this subject. Again, I recommend "*The Body Keeps The Score*" by Bessel van der Kolk M.D. It's a wonderful introduction to trauma and its effects on our lives.

Summary

● Past trauma can cause enormous inner resistance to success. It can result in many self-sabotaging behaviors (like procrastination) and can stop you from moving ahead in life.

- TRE® (Tension and Trauma Releasing Exercises) is one of the best ways to get rid of the trauma that may be the reason behind your procrastination habit.

89. The Simplest Way To Boost Focus & Mental Clarity

The Problem

The human mind is beautifully imperfect. Sometimes, even pumped-up emotions are not enough to make you take action. Sometimes the urge to postpone work overcomes even the strongest motivation.

You know you should go and do what needs to be done, but you make excuses. You procrastinate. You resist taking action.

And motivation doesn't seem to work.

What you need here is the WILLPOWER to take action even if you are not in the mood to do it and the DISCIPLINE to not let yourself get distracted by other things. Both willpower and discipline are very powerful traits by themselves, and their effectiveness multiplies several-fold if you incorporate both in your behavior.

You might say, "That's great, but how the heck I am supposed to develop willpower **AND** discipline?"

The Procrastination Solution

The answer is meditation. Just 10-15 minutes of daily meditation works like MAGIC in developing willpower and discipline.

There is a whole array of scientific research on meditation and its effects.

In her excellent book *'Maximum Willpower'*, Kelly McGonigal states that we have a finite reserve of willpower and discipline. The more you tap into these reserves, the faster they would get drained. Meditation is an actual practice which replenishes these reserves and can even expand them.

Medical research has shown meditation activates and develops the pre-frontal cortex part of our mind which is known to be the command center of behavioral traits like willpower.

Link to study:
https://cursos.isvara.com.br/wp-content/uploads/2020/02/07-Specific-prefrontal-cortical-activation.pdf

In my own personal experience, I have found meditation to be the best and the most effective way to develop willpower and discipline. It's even more effective than taking medical drugs or stimulants for cultivating these two traits.

And as an added bonus, you will experience many other useful benefits including - increased concentration, calmness, relaxation, and happiness, to name just a few.

If you read about the most successful people, celebrities, athletes - who are at the top of their chosen field - all of these people practice and recommend meditation. Katy Perry, Madonna, Hugh Jackman, Oprah Winfrey, Bill Ford, Kobe Bryant, Russell Simmons, and Anthony Robbins all praise meditation as one of the biggest factors in their success.

If you are trying to become successful or going after any goal you want, add 10 minutes of meditation in your day. It is so effective that once you start seeing the benefits, you will never want to stop.

If you have never done meditation before, I have some good news. The practice of meditation is very simple and you won't have to dwell on any of the religious aspects that people associate with meditation.

At its core, meditation is simply a practice of focusing on your breath. That's it. None of the religious associations are necessary for meditation.

Here's an easy step-by-step guide to meditation.

How to meditate?

1. Set an alarm for 10-15 minutes.

2. Sit comfortably on a chair, keeping your back relaxed & upright. Use a cushion if you need to.

3. Close your eyes and start noticing your breath coming in and out. Notice everything about it: when it enters in your nostrils to when it goes in your diaphragm. The movement of your stomach going up and down, etc.

Eventually, your mind will start thinking about something else. You will get lost in your thoughts. You lose focus on your breath and start dwelling on the other thought itself. It's Ok.

4. Whenever you catch yourself focusing on your thoughts instead of being aware of your breath, gently and calmly return to your original focus on your breath.

5. Soon you will lose your focus again and get lost in thoughts. Relax & simply shift your focus back to your breath calmly.

6. Keep doing this for 15 minutes till your alarm rings.

Note: Don't force yourself to keep your mind empty all the time. The mind will think and that's what we want. Actually, willpower gets stronger when you keep shifting your focus from your thoughts to your breath. This 'to and fro' of awareness is what strengthens willpower muscles. It's like a gym for your mind.

Just follow the simple instructions and start doing meditation daily. You will be surprised by the effect on your discipline and willpower level. As a result, you will overcome your excuses and take a lot more action.

Summary

- Practicing meditation will increase your willpower levels. Its effectiveness is documented by studies conducted all across the globe. Our daily life has become so demanding that we end up having a very low reserve of willpower and succumb to procrastination.

- This simple exercise is the answer. It strengthens our willpower and helps us fight against procrastination. It is highly recommended.

90. Deep Breathing Technique For Inner Tranquility

The Problem

The presence of negative emotions is a common reason behind procrastination. You may be feeling anxious, scared, angry, insecure, or depressed at the moment which can prevent you from taking action.

The Procrastination Solution

In the field of *Neuro-linguistic Programming*, there's a principle called "State". It says that our behavior depends on our present mood (*state*). When you are feeling good, you are more likely to take productive or positive action. And when you are feeling bad, you tend to procrastinate and avoid taking action. For example, suppose you need to prepare a report or do a house chore but you're feeling depressed, well while you are in that state, you're more prone to procrastination.

We need to let go of any negative emotions that may be stopping you from taking action. Whether you are feeling depressed, angry, anxious, sad, afraid, or other negative emotions, you could let them go and attain a calm, relaxed, resourceful state. When you feel calm, you're more likely to take action and be productive.

There are a lot of techniques to let go of negative emotions. I like to use a simple breathing exercise. It's easy and quite effective at releasing negative emotions. It calms down the mind and allows you to think rationally.

Here's the step-by-step method:

Step 1: **Sit down and close your eyes.**

Sit down on a comfortable chair. Keep your back upright (use cushions if needed). Keep your hands relaxed on your lap. Be comfortable.

Step 2: **Locate the negative feelings.**

Close your eyes and pay attention to your emotions - how are you feeling right now? Naturally, you will start feeling tenseness in your body due to the presence of negative emotions.

Stay with your negative emotions. Do not fight or suppress them. Just observe them. Be with them.

Now, while observing the negative emotions in your body, try to sense where they are located. Some emotions like anger might be centered around the neck & chest area. Emotions like guilt or fear may be located in the stomach and lower back.

Calmly locate where you feel the presence of negative emotions in your body.

Step 3: **Inhale for a count of six.**

Take a deep breath… inhale. And as you inhale, imagine you are inhaling from the very base of your spine - the bottom of your pelvic bones touching the chair. In yoga, that is called our 'root chakra'. This step is very important.

Root chakra is considered the soothing center of the body. It calms down the nerves and releases negative emotions trapped within.

In this step, imagine that you are breathing from the very bottom of your spine/pelvic bones which is touching the seat of your chair. Imagine your nostrils are down there and you're inhaling from there.

Now with your spine upright and your breaths focused on the bottom of your pelvic bone, take a deep breath for a count of six.

Step 4: **Hold the breath for the count of four.**

Don't exhale immediately. Hold the breath for a count of four.

Step 5: **Slowly exhale through your mouth for the count of seven.**

While exhaling, imagine that all the air is originating from root chakra and rising upwards towards your mouth and leaving your body through your mouth. Starting from the base of the spine, coming up, and leaving the body through the mouth.

Step 6: Hold the breath for the count of 3. Then breathe normally. Relax.

That is the whole breathing process.

- Inhale through the nose for the count of 6
- Hold the breath for a count of 4
- Exhale through the mouth for a count of 7
- Hold the breath for a count of 3.

That is one complete cycle. Repeat the cycle two more times (for a total of three).

It induces a deep relaxation response in the body and releases negative emotions, which is what we want.

Our goal behind the deep breathing exercise is to relax & let go of negative emotions and it works like a charm. No matter how intense your negative emotions are, this breathing exercise will bring immediate relaxation.

The whole process may seem lengthy here, but in practice, you can do three rounds of this breathing exercise in three to five minutes. It may take a few tries at first, but once you get this exercise down, it's quite easy to do.

It is very effective in releasing negative emotions, resulting in a relaxed and calm mind. That's a great state for taking action. You'll be raring to go!

Summary

- Negative emotions stop you from taking productive actions.

- Use the breathing technique to release the negative emotions, calm yourself, and attain a productive state of mind.

91. EFT 101: Abolishing Emotional Impediments To Your Goals

Emotional Freedom Technique (EFT) is another effective technique to release negative emotions that may stop you from taking action. Commonly known as 'tapping', it was introduced by Gary Craig back in 1995.

In EFT, we stimulate Chinese meridian points by tapping them with our fingertips to release negative emotions like fear, anxiety, sadness, stress, disgust, anger and create a deep sense of relaxation. Practitioners of this technique believe that there is a natural flow of energy in the human body and the presence of negative emotions disrupt this flow. Tapping on the meridian points of the body with our fingertips restores this flow and releases the negative emotions.

A Controversial Form of Therapy

Contrary to a lot of positive experiences shared by EFT practitioners, it was regarded as 'pseudoscience' by many. In 2019, a major study was conducted on EFT to verify its effectiveness in controlling negative emotions.

Participants were enrolled in a 4-day workshop conducted at various different locations. After 4 days, they went through comprehensive psychological testing. The results were remarkable. Significant declines were found in the levels of anxiety (−40%), depression (−35%), PTSD (−32%), pain (−57%), and cravings (−74%).

All participants reported an increase in general happiness. Significant improvements were found in Resting Heart Rate (−8%), Cortisol (−37%), Systolic Blood Pressure (−6%), and

Diastolic Blood Pressure (−8%). Positive results were found across the board, indicating the validity of the EFT therapy.

Link to research:
https://www.ncbi.nlm.nih.gov/pmc/articles/PMC6381429/

My Experience With EFT

There will always be naysayers. However, I found EFT to be very effective in regulating negative emotions. I have been using EFT for years now, and here's what I think.

Being able to control your emotions is a superpower. EFT is incredible in that regard. It not only helped me boost my productivity but also made a huge positive impact on all areas of life. It made me a better husband, colleague, writer, son, entrepreneur - and most of all - a better human being.

There are no side-effects of EFT if it's learned from a certified practitioner. I would recommend you learn the process from a certified EFT coach. But in my personal experience, I never had any side-effects and I didn't even learn from a certified EFT practitioner.

Seeing how effective EFT is, I always wondered why it's not getting attention in the mainstream media that it deserves. Why it is still called 'pseudoscience' by many people even if 100's of studies are confirming its validity?

I may never know for sure. But what I do know is that there's a quick & easy way to control my emotions that I can do anywhere, anytime and it will never fail me.

That's all that I wanted to say about EFT. For in-depth information, here's a link to Gary Craig's official website: www.emofree.com
You can check it out if you wish.

92. Trust The Wait. Don't Be Too Hard On Yourself

We are often too hard on ourselves. From our clothes to our make-up, to second guessing what we said to someone three days ago, we spend too much time obsessing over what we could have done "better."

But what does better really mean? I believe that we are too harsh on ourselves, and think that if we achieve this "better," we'll be satisfied. But the reality is different. There's always something "better" that is currently outside our reach.

We struggle to feel content with who we are and what we have. And the truth is, it really doesn't benefit us in the long run to constantly be telling ourselves that we aren't living up to our own expectations.

It is good to push yourself. It is important to have goals, dreams, and aspirations. These keep us going in life! They keep us motivated and excited. They energize us. But the problem comes when we push too hard and when we forget to compliment ourselves, and get lost in the constant demands of perfection.

We need to be more forgiving of ourselves. We need to pay respect to how many things we are doing; how many responsibilities we are trying to fulfil. We honestly need to cut ourselves some slack.

We are SO much harder on ourselves than we are on anyone else. We are our own worst critics, but not our own best supporters. And because we don't celebrate our victories, or be grateful for what we already have, we tend to forget how incredibly valuable we are.

We think the little things are so important. We hyperfocus on anything that causes us anxiety and we put ourselves down for things that will not even matter in the long run. We become so concerned with being the best that we can, that we end up thinking that we are not enough.

This brings me to believe that we need to be a little more gentle with ourselves. It's okay to procrastinate. We all need to start to realize that we are doing the best we can, no matter what it looks like to us or to others. We are all trying to succeed. We are all trying to be good people. We are all trying to do what is right – that is the truth.

However, you are human. You can't always be perfect. You rise, and you fall. That's life. So, try to appreciate the small stuff. Celebrate the accomplishments as you go, take some time off to acknowledge how far you've come in your quest to overcome procrastination.

Do not judge or criticize yourself harshly. You've already accepted that you procrastinate on important work, that's a major step in the right direction. Follow the advice in this book and you're surely going to overcome it.

And even if you make fumbles along the way, it is okay.

Listen to me.

It is okay.

It's all right to make mistakes. If you fall, get up, dust yourself off, and try again.

In the end, it's all that matters.

Parting Thoughts

Thank you for purchasing this book.

The key to great success, satisfaction, and joy lies in becoming the most productive version of yourself.

The good news is that this is a learnable skill that you can develop via practice. And once you master the art of getting started and maintaining consistency, success is inevitable.

As I mentioned earlier, this book is meant to be used as a reference guide. Any time you need a refresher or solution to a specific problem, come back and re-read the related section.

In your journey to master productivity, you would enviably come across various obstacles. Any time you feel stuck, remember not to get discouraged. You only need a new skill or information.

For instance, if you can successfully get started on the tasks, but are having problems maintaining consistency, then refer to Section-II that deals with this issue.

Please remember, there's always a way around your problem. Make a life-long commitment to keep a student's mindset and never stop learning & growing.

It feels great to find solutions and overcome the challenges that you are facing. It's a very liberating feeling.

Once you figured out how to solve a problem, you never have to worry about it again. It's like finding a combination of a lock. Once you find it, you are good for life.

As you do this, you will experience massive amounts of success, and as a spill-over effect, you become a lot more confident in your everyday life.

Can you imagine how confident you would be when you know there is always a way around problems and you can find it?

Success is quite similar to the stock market. The more you put in, the more you shall receive. And if you work smart, you might receive more than what you put in.

Careful planning and execution are crucial if you want to reach the next level in your finance, health, and success. A few people believe they reached the pinnacle. There is nothing more.

I believe there is always the next level. No matter how skilled you may become, there is always a chance to grow.

Stop looking at your competitors and the people around you.

Compete only with yourself. No one else. The only challenge you should be looking to beat is your own limit.

Always keep growing and improving yourself. Never stop.

This world needs you to be your best self.

By being your best, you will inspire other people to do the same. Become a pillar of positivity and strength for your society.

Think of how much good you can do for others when you have the time and energy to do so.

Obtaining success is not selfish. It's your right. It's the best thing you can do to make this world a better place.

I wish you all the success, love, and happiness that you truly deserve.

Thank you.

Max.

Let me know your thoughts.

I want to know what you are thinking. Your thoughts and ideas are important to me. **I would be grateful if you'd post a short review on Amazon**. Your support makes a significant difference. I read all reviews myself so that I can gather your feedback and make improvements to the book.

Your support is deeply appreciated!

About the Author

Max Goldwall is a high-performance and productivity coach, entrepreneur, and author.

He has worked with people from various cultures and ethnicities for more than a decade to help them become more productive and successful.

His mission is to revolutionize how work is perceived and drive a new era of development, growth, and productivity.

He has a post-graduate degree in business management. Besides coaching and writing, he likes meditation, yoga, nutrition, reading, and traveling.

You can contact him at:

Email:
yourselfactualization@gmail.com

Facebook group:
https://www.facebook.com/groups/727799514578811

Your Free eBook: *Small Habits* by Max Goldwall

Small Habits is a groundbreaking book about breaking bad habits and building good ones. It is designed to help you transition from *procrastination* to *productivity* and make the changes permanent.

To download the eBook at no cost, please join our productivity Facebook group by clicking on the link below:

https://www.facebook.com/groups/727799514578811

www.ingramcontent.com/pod-product-compliance
Lightning Source LLC
Chambersburg PA
CBHW020627220526
45464CB00001B/52